D0705899

Reasoning and the Law

THE ELEMENTS

Elias E. Savellos
State University of New York at Genesco

with **Richard F. Galvin**
Texas Christian University

 **Wadsworth**
Thomson Learning™

Australia • Canada • Mexico • Singapore • Spain • United Kingdom • United States

Philosophy Editor: Peter Adams
Assistant Editor: Kerri Abdinoor
Editorial Assistant: Mark Andrews
Marketing Manager: Dave Garrison
Print Buyer: Mary Noel
Permissions Editor: Bob Kauser
Production Service: Gustafson Graphics

Copy Editor: Linda Ireland
Cover Designer: Ross Carron
Cover Image: © PhotoDisc Inc.
Cover Printer: Webcom Limited
Signing Representative: Michelle Witcher
Compositor: Gustafson Graphics
Printer/Binder: Webcom Limited

Printed in Canada
1   2   3   4   5   6   7   03   02   01

For permission to use material from this text, contact us by
    Web: http://www.thomsonrights.com
    Fax: 1-800-730-2215
    Phone: 1-800-730-2214

For more information, contact
Wadsworth/Thomson Learning
10 Davis Drive
Belmont, CA 94002-3098
USA

http://www.wadsworth.com
International Headquarters
Thomson Learning
International Division
290 Harbor Drive, 2nd Floor
Stamford, CT 06902-7477
USA

UK/Europe/Middle East/South Africa
Thomson Learning
Berkshire House
168-173 High Holborn
London WC1V 7AA
United Kingdom

Asia
Thomson Learning
60 Albert Street, #15-01
Albert Complex
Singapore 189969

Canada
Nelson Thomson Learning
1120 Birchmount Road
Toronto, Ontario M1K 5G4
Canada

Library of Congress Cataloging-in-Publication Data
Savellos, Elias E.
    Reasoning and the law : the elements / Elias E. Savellos & Richard F. Galvin.
        p. cm.
    Includes bibliographical references.
    ISBN 0-534-53895-9
        1. Law—Methodology.   2. Law—Interpretation and construction.   3. Logic.
    4. Reasoning.   I. Galvin, Richard F.   II. Title.
K213.S28 2000
340'.1—dc21   00-022851

CONTENTS

Part II   Elements of Legal Reasoning   57

Chapter 3   **Reasoning and the Law   59**

Part III   Case Analysis   85

Chapter 4   **Guidelines for Analyzing Cases   87**

INTRODUCTION

In this book we provide a step-by-step introduction to those elements of reasoning, and legal reasoning in particular, that are of fundamental importance to those who are just beginning the exploration of the legal field. The book is divided into three closely related parts. In part I we present a comprehensive and accessible section on those elements of logic and reasoning that, in our opinion, are indispensable for the rigorous study of law. In part II we address the application of reasoning in legal contexts and in judicial decisions in particular. In part III we provide a hands-on application of the material encountered in previous chapters through the detailed analysis of two well-known judicial cases.

There are several unique features in this book:

- **Narrowly targeted coverage of logic:** Standard textbooks in critical thinking, logic, and reasoning are designed for use in general, full-length logic and/or critical thinking courses. These are courses that, traditionally, place heavy emphasis on symbolism, formal methods for assessing validity, or, at the other end, the countless ways we can commit "informal fallacies." Thus they tend to cover much more ground than the pre-law undergraduate actually needs. By contrast, our book is written with an eye to the specific, narrower needs of the undergraduate student who finds herself enrolled in a pre-law course that demands a good grasp of elementary logico-analytical techniques. Thus we discuss just those matters that, we believe, constitute basic, essential background for dealing effectively with complex argumentative legal material.
- **Legal reasoning for *pre-law* students:** As anyone who starts exploring the law immediately realizes, a good understanding of reasoning in general and of legal reasoning in particular is hardly an option for those who are interested in the study of the field. Yet standard textbooks in logic and reasoning again fall short in that they do not address the special nature of legal reasoning and judicial decision making. On the other hand, available texts in "legal reasoning" are geared toward the *law-school student,* the professional lawyer, the philosopher of law, or the theorist of jurisprudence—in short, anyone but the beginning *pre-law* student. In our book we attempt to remedy this situation. We provide a brief, nontechnical introduction to legal reasoning that is geared toward *undergraduates,* not first-year law students.
- **Integration of logic and law:** From the beginning sections to the very end, we attempt to apply the tools of logic to actual law cases. We derive all our examples, practice questions, exercises, and applications from legal contexts. And in the last part of this work we show students how the elements of logic and legal reasoning they learn in this book come together to yield coherent, justified judicial decisions.

- **Student-friendly exposition:** We have aimed at producing a book that students can use with minimal involvement of the instructor. We have kept "technical" material and points to a bare minimum, and we have incorporated a series of pedagogical aids. The latter include: a nontechnical, nonsymbolic review of basic logical concepts; detailed indexing of content for easy reference; extensive cross-referencing; frequent use of tips and warnings on applying methods and techniques; graphic devices; sample applications of the material including the detailed analysis of two judicial cases; practice and "to think about" questions; and self-diagnostic tests with answers. We have also provided two important appendices: a brief, bird's-eye overview of the legal environment, and a practical guide on writing argumentative papers (a must for the student of law).

We believe that these features will enable this book to be used in a wide variety of contexts. It is ideally suited to introduce logic and legal reasoning to those with limited analytical skills and no prior exposure to these matters. Yet it can also be used as a refresher of the most basic and law-related concepts and tools by those students who already have had a "standard" logic background. Moreover, it can provide crucial help to those taking the LSAT, and it can provide essential information to anyone interested in law and the nature and process of the judicial decision.

To be sure, there are at least two distinct settings in which this book should find a natural home. First, it can be used as the basic text in undergraduate **legal reasoning courses.** These courses *par excellence* prepare undergraduates interested in the law for what to expect from the systematic study of the field, namely, lots of reasoned decisions, argumentation, and extensive application of logical tools and techniques. Moreover, they provide an excellent opportunity for those interested in the law to test whether they have "the right stuff" for the pursuit of a law-related career.

Second, this book can be used as a supplementary text in those **pre-law courses that demand rigorous understanding and employment of fundamental logical tools and techniques** (for example, philosophy of law). Many students who enroll in such courses lack the requisite background that would enable them to cope effectively with the rigorous material they encounter. Thus they face serious difficulties when they are called to conduct a detailed analysis of a judicial opinion or to dissect complex argumentative legal texts. As a result many aspiring law-bound students are often disappointed by what erroneously seems to them a field that lies outside their critical abilities. Unfortunately, the available reading resources in the field do not remedy the situation. Anthologies of pre-law material, or even so-called "introductory texts," do not provide students with the skills they need to tackle complex argumentative legal texts. And, as already indicated, available legal reasoning texts aim too high, while standard logic texts require a course of study on their own. We hope that when the present book is put to use (as a supplementary text) in these courses, it will remedy the situation: instructors will be able to concentrate on the main material of their course, while students will have a handy aid for their basic logic needs.

ACKNOWLEDGMENTS

In writing this book we have benefited from the generous assistance of several individuals. In the first place, we wish to thank a group of colleagues who reviewed earlier drafts of the manuscript and offered comments that considerably improved the book: Hugo Bedau, Tufts University; Raymond Bellioti, State University of New York, College of Fredonia; Andrew Buchwalter, University of North Florida; Harvey Cormier, University of Texas at Austin; Kai Draper, Kansas State University; Stephen Esquith, Michigan State University; Joel Feinberg, The University of Arizona; Thaddeus Metz, University of Missouri, St. Louis; and Nancy Snow, Marquette University. In the second place, a special thanks goes to Julia Calnek who patiently read the final manuscript and offered several insightful editorial and substantive suggestions. Similarly, we are indebted to our Editor, Peter Adams for his help and encouragement throughout. Additionally, and most importantly, we owe an enormous emotional debt to our families for their generous and continuous support. Finally, this book is dedicated to Vivian, *sine qua non*.

PART I

ELEMENTS OF REASONING

CHAPTER 1

STATEMENTS

1.1 WORDS

The smallest units of meaningful, natural language are words. Technicalities aside, it is important to see that we normally distinguish two aspects of meaningful words: what sorts of things they are about (what they refer to), and what their cognitive significance is (what they mean). That is, for a given word *W*, we distinguish between the reference and the meaning of *W*:

> The **reference** (extension, denotation, designation) of *W* is the range of application of *W*, the class of all the *things* (past, present, and future) that *W* applies to. Thus, for example, the word *attorney* refers to (denotes, designates) all and only past, present, and future attorneys.

> The **meaning** (intention, connotation) of *W* is the cognitive significance conveyed by *W*. Usually, this is captured by conveying the class of all the *characteristics* that are shared by the things that are in the extension of *W*. The meaning of *judge,* for example, is given by listing the characteristics that judges possess—such attributes as being duly appointed to a judicial position, having the authority to hear cases, rule on motions, hold people in contempt, and so on.

1.1.1 Reference and Singular versus General Terms

Some terms are used to refer to one and only one thing. Proper names (for example, *Elias, Richard*), definite descriptions (for example, *the current President of the U.S.*), and demonstratives (for example, *this, that*) have this function; hence they are called **singular terms.** Other terms are **general,** in that they are used to refer to all the members of a class. Words such as *judge, court, president,* and *murder* are like that.

1.2 MEANING AND DEFINITION

The meaning of a word can be cashed out in several ways, but the most common and fruitful way is to produce a definition of it. To define a word *W* is to provide another word or group of words that captures what we do or should understand by *W*. For example, we might define the word *attorney* by using the single word *lawyer,* or by a set of words, as in "a person qualified to practice law." In technical but commonly encountered language, the word that is defined is the *definiendum,* and the word(s) that does the defining is the *definiens.* Before we go on, however, we need to bring to your attention two sources of concern: ambiguity and vagueness.

1.2.1 Ambiguity and Vagueness

Ambiguity Sometimes when we look up some word *W* in a dictionary, we find not just one meaning of it but *several.* Of course, there is nothing wrong with a word *W* being used in ordinary speech in many different ways. Most words have more than one meaning. What can be a problem, however, is that sometimes the *context* where *W* occurs does not make it clear which of the different meanings of *W* is the intended one. Consider, for example, the word *court.* First, there are meanings of *court* that are unrelated to the law (for example, a building's courtyard, the place of residence of a sovereign, where tennis games are played, rituals of courtship). Second, even within the narrower sense of "court of law," if we go to any decent dictionary we will find at least three different meanings of *court:* (a) a *person(s)* authorized to decide legal cases; (b) a *place* where legal cases are decided; (c) a *session* or meeting of adjudicators. But then how should we understand the sentence "This issue requires a court decision"?

What we have here is a case of *ambiguity.* It should be obvious that no term is ambiguous in isolation. Ambiguity always occurs in a specific *context* in which a term that has several distinct meanings is used. To summarize these remarks:

> **Ambiguity** A term *W* is ambiguously used in a given context when that context does not make it clear which of the several meanings of *W* is the intended one.

Vagueness Sometimes we are clear about the meaning of a term *W* (including which of the several meanings of *W* is intended), yet we are not sure whether the term correctly applies to a given case. Consider, for example, the word *vehicle.* There is no doubt that this term applies to automobiles. But does it apply to skateboards and roller skates? And what of airplanes? (Whether the meaning of *vehicle* as specified in the National Motor Vehicle Theft Act applies to aircraft was the key issue in the well-known *McBoyle v. United States,* 283 U.S. 25 (1931).) The answer is not clear; the term *vehicle* is a *vague* term. Let us give a working understanding of this linguistic phenomenon:

> **Vagueness** A term *W* is vague when there is a "gray area" of applicability of *W;* there are borderline cases in which it is not clearly determined that they fall under *W.*

The attentive reader should have already detected from what has been said that most words exhibit some vagueness. But this does not make vagueness unmanageable. First notice that vagueness is not an all-or-nothing affair, but rather a matter of degree. Some words (for example, *bald, rich, intelligent*) are quite "fuzzy" in that they display a great degree of vagueness. Others (for example, *Internet, jury*) are less vague (if at all), and yet others (for example, *criminal*) seem to be entirely free of vagueness (whether or not *criminal* applies to a given case seems to be a matter that can be decided in an "on/off" fashion given the criminal law). Nonetheless, we cannot avoid vagueness entirely, since, on pain of silence, we cannot be absolutely precise all the time. But we can avoid using highly vague words, and strive for a degree of precision that is sufficient to communicate clearly what we wish to communicate in a given context. Second, in contexts that matter, we do have ways of dealing with undesirable vagueness, for example, we can provide definitions.

A final word before we move on. A term can be both vague and ambiguous. Terms like *right, death,* and *official* are just like that. We deal with them by making use of definitions.

Sample Application

A Case of Vagueness   In the well-known case of *McBoyle v. United States,* 283 U.S. 25 (1931), McBoyle was accused of interstate transportation of a stolen airplane in violation of a federal statute that prohibited transportation of stolen *motor vehicles* across state lines. The issue was whether an airplane counts as a motor vehicle; if so he violated the statute, if not he did not violate it. The statute provided that: "The term 'motor vehicle' shall include an automobile, automobile truck, automobile wagon, motorcycle, *or any other self-propelled vehicle not designed for running on rails*" (emphasis added). The clause in italics in the previous sentence is vague. The problem is that an airplane does not "run on rails" because it does not "run" *on* anything—it *flies.* So given the list of items that the statute stipulates as vehicles, should the airplane be considered a vehicle or not? The trial court convicted McBoyle, but the Supreme Court reversed the conviction by holding that the meaning of *vehicle* as specified in the above-emphasized clause of the statute does not apply to aircraft.

A Case of Ambiguity   In Nix v. Hedden, 149 U.S. 304 (1893), the Supreme Court was called to decide whether tomato means "fruit" or "vegetable." The Court reasoned that "There being no evidence that the words 'fruit' and 'vegetables' have acquired any special meaning in trade or commerce, they must receive their ordinary meaning." Thus Justice Gray decided that though "botanically speaking" tomatoes can be classified as fruits of a vine, the ordinary usage of the term in everyday language shows that tomatoes are understood to be vegetables after all. Although one might be tempted to dismiss this as an exercise in verbal hair-splitting, such decisions can have important implications. We can easily imagine regulations that apply to fruit but not vegetables, and vice versa. And the Reagan administration once claimed that ketchup should count as a vegetable in school lunch programs.

1.2.2 Kinds of Definitions

There are several different kinds of definitions, depending on what criteria of classification are used. We examine here just three kinds that are particularly relevant to the law:

- Reportive (lexical) definitions
- Stipulative definitions
- Precising definitions

1.2.2.1 Reportive (Lexical) Definitions
When we ask for the definition of a word *W* whose meaning we do not know, the first thing that seems to come to mind is a good dictionary. Why? Because dictionaries define *W* by explaining how *W* is actually used in the language. Since such a definition reports the ordinary meaning of *W,* the meaning that *W* already has, we call it a *reportive* (or *lexical*) definition. A good reportive definition must accurately (truly) report the actual, customary way we ordinarily understand *W,* and we are entitled to criticize the definition if it fails in this task.

1.2.2.2 Stipulative Definitions
It is often useful or convenient to introduce a brand-new term *W* into our vocabulary, and stipulate that from this point on *W* will have the special meaning we say it has. In this case, we have a *stipulative* definition for *W.* Stipulative definitions are common in the law. When a proposed statute, for example, employs for the first time unusual terminology, say *Internet donee,* the legislators are free to stipulate at will how we are to understand this term from now on. Thus if they define it as "a person who uses HTML language to post his/her will on the Internet," then that is what is meant by *Internet donee.* Thus a stipulative definition is a tool of convenience, and we are not entitled to criticize it as false, produce counterexamples to it, or reject it on the grounds that this is not the way ordinary people would have used the definiendum. Indeed, the need for a stipulative definition usually arises because there is no clearly established, customary usage already in place.

1.2.2.3 Precising Definitions
In discussing vagueness we observed that in several ordinary situations, we can successfully communicate what we want despite using vague words. In some contexts, however, precision is a must. For example, the term *death* carries a degree of vagueness that is intolerable in some contexts where the stakes are high. Still, if someone is dying, many important procedural and legal decisions need to be made. When we deal with matters of abortion and euthanasia, for example, it is imperative that we carefully define what precisely will count as death. Thus in these contexts, our best weapon against the vagueness of ordinary terms is a *precising* definition.

To give a precising definition is to take an ordinary word that has (a) a well-established usage, but (b) a fuzzy range of applicability, and specify that in a specific context the word will be understood to mean precisely what we say it will mean. Thus, for example, the National Motor Vehicle Theft Act provides: "Sec. 2. That when used in this Act: (a) The term 'motor vehicle' shall include an automobile, automobile truck, automobile wagon, motorcycle, or any other self-propelled vehicle not designed for running on rails."

Precising definitions are quite common in the law. Indeed, we are all painfully familiar with the excessive occurrence of legal terminology and precising definitions in statutes, administrative rules, and formal contracts. This is neither an accident nor the result of love of wordiness. The stakes are simply too high to leave certain matters in a shadow of uncertainty.

To Think About

Can you classify the following definitions?

Homeless means an individual who lacks a fixed, regular, and adequate nighttime residence (U.S.C. tit. 42, ch. 119).

Photographs include still photographs, x-rays, film, videotapes, and motion pictures (Federal Rules of Evidence 10,001).

The term "standards of performance" means a standard for emissions of air pollutants which reflects the degree of emission limitation achievable through the application of the best system of emission reduction (taking into account the cost of achieving such reduction and any non-air quality health and environmental impact and energy requirements the Administration [of the Environmental Protection Agency] determines has been adequately demonstrated) (Federal Clean Air Act, § 111(a)(1)).

The term "person" means an individual, a corporation, a partnership, an association, a joint-stock company, a trust, any unincorporated organization, or a government or political subdivision thereof. As used in this paragraph the term "trust" shall include only a trust where the interest or interests of the beneficiary or beneficiaries are evidenced by a security (U.S.C. tit. 15, ch. 2A, subch. I, § 77b(a)(2)).

Test Your Knowledge #1

Answer "true" or "false." (If you get less than 90% correct, go back and reread. The answers are at the end of part I.)

_____ 1. The extension of a term *w* consists of the characteristics that are shared by the things that are denoted by *w*.

_____ 2. The intention of a term *w* is the class of all things that *w* applies to.

_____ 3. The term *president of the U.S.* is a singular term.

_____ 4. The *definiendum* is the expression that does the defining.

_____ 5. The term *liquid* is ambiguous.

_____ 6. The term *bald* is vague.

_____ 7. The term *rich* is both vague and ambiguous.

_____ 8. The following is a stipulative definition: "*Intoxicated* for purposes of driving a car in many states means having a blood-alcohol ratio of 1 to .001 or greater."

_____ 9. A stipulative definition is either true or false.

_____ 10. A lexical definition reports the way a word is actually used in a language.

1.3 SENTENCES, LANGUAGE USES, AND TRUTH

We use words to form sentences, the basic units of verbal communication. We put these sentences to many uses, and pursue many goals in doing so. For instance, we ask questions, give commands, make promises, make excuses, apologize, condemn, praise, joke, express our emotions, greet people, curse, pray, sing, and give information.

In each of these cases the main concern is to use language to achieve some purpose. Notice, however, that the issue of the truth or falsity of what has been said does not always arise. That is, it may not always make sense for a critical mind to ask whether the sentence the speaker has uttered is true or false (*A:* "What time is it?"; *B:* "Ha! What you said is false").

On the other hand, our sentences often have what logicians call a truth value, and it then makes sense to ask whether what has been said is true or false. In this case we will say that we have a *claim* or a *statement:*

> **Claim** (or **Statement**)   A sentence about which it makes sense to ask whether it is true or false.

Claims are the "the stuff of logic," the focus of attention in reasoning. From this point on we will be concerned primarily with statements.

1.3.1 Kinds of Statements

Statements can be classified in several ways. In this section we examine four pairs of "opposite" statements that are particularly useful for the study of law. These are:

- Necessary versus contingent
- Normative versus descriptive
- Singular versus categorical
- Simple versus compound

1.3.1.1 Necessary versus Contingent

Consider the following pair of statements:

1. Clarence Thomas is a Supreme Court judge.

2. Either Clarence Thomas is a judge or Clarence Thomas is not a judge.

Although each of these statements is true, there is an important difference between them. One way to see the difference is to consider the type of information conveyed by each. Statement 1 is informative. It tells us that as a matter of fact things are in a certain way: there is some person named Clarence Thomas who, as it happens, is a Supreme Court judge. On the other hand, statement 2 seems "empty" in that it does not seem to convey any new information at all. To put the same point slightly differently: if a question about the truth of statement 1 arises, the issue can be decided by conducting a quick empirical investigation (for example, we ask at the Supreme Court, call a newspaper, get on the Internet, and so on). By contrast, the truth of statement 2 is independent of empirical investigation; it is obvious to anyone who understands (a) the meaning of the English words in it, as well as (b) some very basic principles of logic (imagine how they would laugh if you called the Supreme Court and asked whether statement 2 is true!). Statements (like 1) whose truth value depends upon facts about the world are called *contingent* or *a posteriori*, or *synthetic*. Statements (like 2) whose truth value depends on language and logic alone are called *necessary*, or *a priori*, or *analytic*. Contingent statements *may* be true or *may* be false, depending on how the world actually is. Necessary statements *must* be either always true or always false. A necessary statement that is always true is a *tautology*. A necessary statement that is always false ("Clarence Thomas is a judge and he is not a judge") is a *contradiction*.

ᎶᏅ   **A Point of Detail**   This classification of statements into two groups (the contingent/a posteriori/synthetic group and the necessary/a priori/analytic group) is neither as simple nor as uncontroversial as it may at first look. From the famous eighteenth-century philosopher Immanuel Kant, who argued that there are synthetic a priori statements, to the twentieth-century philosopher W.V.O. Quine, who argued that there are no analytic statements, these distinctions have been a matter of heated dispute. Most recently, philosopher Saul Kripke proposed that the analytic/synthetic distinction is a linguistic one, the contingent /necessary distinction is a matter of metaphysics, and the a priori/a posteriori distinction concerns the way we know the truth of a statement. Kripke also argued that there are statements (for example, "Water is H_2O") that are necessary (in the sense that the world could not be otherwise now that it is the way it is) and a posteriori (in the sense that we know their truth value as a matter of empirical discovery). Prior to Kripke's work it was generally held that necessary truths must be knowable a priori.

1.3.1.2 Normative versus Descriptive

There is an important difference between the following two statements:

1. Sometimes people disobey the law.
2. People ought to obey the laws.

Statement 1 *describes* the world. It tells us (truly or falsely) that it is a fact that people violate laws. Statement 2, by contrast, does not convey any information about how things are (it makes no claim about whether people do or do not obey laws), but rather *prescribes* how things ought to be. Statements like 1 are called *descriptive,* and statements like 2, which involve such prescriptive words as *ought, should,* and their cognates, are called *normative.* Normative statements play a crucial role in our theorizing about many important human institutions, perhaps most notably ethics, religion, and law.

1.3.1.3 Singular versus Categorical

Some statements are *singular* in that they are about a single thing or situation. The following are examples:

1. The Supreme Court rules on the constitutionality of statutes.
2. O. J. Simpson has been found not guilty of criminal charges.
3. The death penalty is cruel and unusual punishment.

By contrast, *categorical* statements are statements about classes (or categories) of things or situations. They assert that a particular class is either in part or as a whole related to another class. Let *S* and *P* denote two different classes. Since Aristotle's time logicians have distinguished four "standard" patterns or forms of relation that might hold between classes *S* and *P.* These are given below along with an example of each:

PATTERN	EXAMPLE
All *S* are *P*	All the jurors in the O. J. Simpson trial were U.S. citizens.
No *S* are *P*	No foreign nationals are eligible to serve as president.
Some *S* are *P*	Some decisions of the Supreme Court are controversial.
Some *S* are not *P*	Some attorneys are not Harvard graduates.

The first pattern tells us that all the members of the *S* class are also members of the *P* class. That is, class *S* is totally included within the *P* class. In the example of this first pattern the statement asserts that the entire class consisting of persons who were jurors in the O. J. Simpson trial is included in the class of U.S. citizens. And the statement would be true if all the jurors were indeed U.S. citizens.

The second pattern tells us that classes *S* and *P* are wholly excluded from each other, that is, classes *S* and *P* have no members in common. Thus the example of this pattern tells us that the entire class of persons who are foreign nationals is excluded from the class of persons who are eligible for the presidency. This claim would be true if foreign nationals are indeed ineligible for the office of president.

The third pattern gives us a relation of partial inclusion. It tells us that some members of the *S* class ("some" for logicians means "at least one") are also members of the *P* class. Thus the example of this pattern states that part (that is, at least one member) of the class of Supreme Court decisions is also included in the class of controversial decisions. This statement is true as long as at least one Supreme Court decision is controversial.

The fourth and final pattern is one of partial exclusion. It tells us that at least one member of the *S* class is not a member of the *P* class. Thus the example statement asserts that there is at least one member of the class of attorneys who does not belong to the class of Harvard graduates. And as long as at least one attorney is not a Harvard graduate, this statement is true.

1.3.1.4 Simple versus Compound

A *simple* statement is one that does not contain any other statement as a component. The following are examples of simple statements:

1. Jury duty is a citizen's obligation.
2. Clinton's impeachment proceedings were closely watched by many people.
3. Clinton is the fifty-fourth U.S. president.

A *compound* statement is one that contains at least one simple statement as a component. For example, consider the following:

4. Bill Clinton is the president of the U.S., and Al Gore is the vice president of the U.S.

This statement is a compound of the simpler statements "Bill Clinton is the president" and "Al Gore is the vice-president."

The following is a more complex compound statement:

5. If Congress passes the bill and the statute is enacted, then either the citizens will revolt or the courts will refuse to enforce the statute.

This is a compound of the simple statements "Congress passes the bill," "the statute is enacted," "the citizens will revolt," and "the courts will refuse to enforce the statute)." The expressions "if . . . then . . .," "and," "either . . . or . . .," connect together these simple statements and form the longer compound that is statement 5. But we are now entering into some very central matters in logic that merit closer examination.

TEST YOUR KNOWLEDGE #2

Answer "true" or "false." (If you get less than 90% correct, go back and reread. The answers are at the end of part I.)

_____ 1. Questions and commands have a truth value.

_____ 2. A claim is a sentence that is either true or false.

_____ 3. Statements whose truth is grounded on language and logic alone are analytic.

_____ 4. A necessary statement that is always true is a tautology.

_____ 5. "Criminals should go to jail" is a normative statement.

_____ 6. "J. C. is not a criminal" is a singular statement.

_____ 7. "All *S* are *P*" is a categorical statement.

_____ 8. "Some criminals do not get the death penalty" is a categorical statement.

_____ 9. "Either J. C. is a criminal or he is not" is a simple statement.

_____ 10. "J. R. is unquestionably one of the most brilliant judges who will make history with his judicial opinions" is a compound statement.

1.3.2 Truth-Functional Compounds

Compound statements receive much attention in logic. They are logically interesting in their own right, and they also provide a valuable tool for the analysis and evaluation of arguments, perhaps the main concern of logicians. How so? The answer is that many logical "calculations," including the evaluation of arguments, are generated by focusing exclusively on truth values. But as it turns out, the truth values of many compound statements can be figured out in easy and helpful ways. We must look more closely at the kinds of compound that are of special interest. These are:

- Conjunctions
- Disjunctions
- Conditionals
- Biconditionals
- Negations

1.3.2.1 Conjunctions

These are formed with the word *and* or one of its cognates (for example, *but, although, also, yet, however, still,* and so on). Thus, for example, the sentence

1. J. C. was found not guilty in the criminal trial, and J. C. was held liable in the civil trial.

is a conjunction whose component parts are the simple statements "J. C. was found not guilty in the criminal trial" and "J. C. was held liable in the civil trial."

But what is the truth value of the *whole compound* statement above? The answer is "it depends on the truth values of the simple statements that are its components." Indeed, it seems obvious that the whole compound statement 1 will be true only when *both* simple sentences that are its components are true, and it will be false in any other case. That is, the answer to our question about the truth value of statement 1 is this: If both component statements "J. C. was found not guilty in the criminal trial" and "J. C. was held liable in the civil trial" are true, then the compound statement 1 is true. If either or both of the component statements are false, then 1 is false. The truth value of 1, it turns out, is a function of the truth values of the component parts. This is why logicians refer to a conjunction such as statement 1 as a *truth-functional compound.* We can generalize:

> For any two statements *A* and *B*, the **conjunction** *"A* and *B"* is true when and only when *both* component statements *A, B* are true. Otherwise it is false.

It is crucial to note that since *A* and *B* stand for any two statements, the boxed text represents the truth conditions for any conjunction whatsoever. That is, *A* and *B* are "placeholders," meant to stand for or represent *any* statement whatsoever. Since *A* and *B* represent any two statements, it follows that the conjunction of *any* two statements, *no matter what those statements are,* will be true just in case each of the two statements is itself true.

1.3.2.2 Disjunctions
These are formed with the word "or" or one of its cognates (for example, *either . . . or . . ., unless*). Thus, for example, the statement

1. Either Johnny Cochran cross-examined Mark Fuhrman or F. Lee Bailey cross-examined Mark Fuhrman.

is a disjunctive compound that includes the simple statements "Johnnie Cochran cross-examined Mark Fuhrman" and "F. Lee Bailey cross-examined Mark Fuhrman." What are the truth conditions of this compound statement? Just as with conjunctions earlier, we can present synoptically the truth conditions of any disjunction whatsoever as follows:

> For any two statements *A* and *B*, the **disjunction** *"A* or *B"* is false when and only when *both* component statements *A, B* are false. Otherwise it is true.

Notice that this tells us that a disjunction is true when *both* components are true. This is the so-called "inclusive" sense of disjunction, a sense that corresponds roughly to "this or that *and perhaps both.*" Thus, for example, the ordinary statement "show a passport or valid driver's license" is meant inclusively, since it surely does not hurt if you show both. A moment's reflection will reveal that statement 1 above is an inclusive disjunction—it is possible that *both* Cochran and Bailey cross-examined Fuhrman, and the statement is clearly consistent with that possibility. Some disjunctions, nonetheless, are meant "exclusively" as "one or the other *but not both.*" Thus, for example, when we read "soup or salad" on a restaurant's menu, we are definitely supposed to understand that we can have either soup or salad but we cannot have both. Again, in "Either the Dodgers or the Giants will play in this year's World Series," the disjunction is clearly exclusive, since both teams are in the National League and only one team will win the National League pennant. In general, ordinary discourse provides no strict guidelines about whether a given disjunction is inclusive or exclusive, but this is not a serious concern from a logical point of view. For reasons that need not concern us here, in logic one can safely rely on using only the inclusive sense of disjunction.

1.3.2.3 Conditionals

Consider the following statements:

1. *If* J. C. gets married again, then J. C. will have a spouse.
2. *If Roe v. Wade* is overturned, *then* the states will have more leeway to restrict abortion.
3. *If* J. C.'s book sells well, *then* he will be able to pay his creditors.

All of these statements are *conditionals,* that is, compounds that share the common form "if _____, then _____" where the blanks are filled by simple statements. The statement that fills in the first blank—that is, the blank that follows the word *if,*—is called the *antecedent* of the conditional. The statement that fills in the second blank, the one after the word *then,* is called the *consequent* of the conditional.

♦ᐩ **Caution**   It is very important to understand these terms and to know in any given case which statement is the antecedent and which is the consequent. For *unlike* other compounds we examine here, the order of appearance of the component parts of a conditional is an all-important matter.

Each of the above conditionals seems to express some kind of connection between the antecedent and the consequent. Yet there are some important differences between the types of connection that each implies. With statement 1 the connection between "J. C. is unmarried" and "J. C. is a bachelor" seems to be definitional or logical. It is a matter simply of the meanings of the terms *spouse* and *married*—to be married is to have a spouse. Statement 2 seems to express a factual or causal connection. Finally, with statement 3 there might be some temporal relationship that is implied between the antecedent and the consequent. Does this mean that the logic of conditionals will differ from case to case? The answer is no: logicians have discovered that whatever their differences, all conditionals have one thing in common—they all assert that *it cannot be that the antecedent is true and yet the consequent is false.* The same point can be put this way: all conditionals assert that *if the antecedent is true, then the consequent **must be** true.* This feature, logicians believe, provides all that is needed to express the truth conditions of all conditionals. We have, then, the following truth conditions for conditionals:

> For any two statements *A* and *B*, the **conditional** "If *A* then *B*" is false when and only when the *antecedent* statement *A* is *true* and the *consequent* statement *B* is *false.* Otherwise it is true.

It may initially appear puzzling that a conditional is true in every case except one—namely, where the antecedent is true and the consequent is false—for this implies that a conditional that has a false antecedent as well as a false consequent is still true! It must be emphasized, however, that the truth conditions presented here exclusively express the truth conditions of what logicians call *truth-functional* (material) *implication.* That is, we express here only the truth value (as opposed to causal or temporal) relationship of the component members of the "if ___, then ___" logical compound and nothing more. And in any case, logicians are not troubled by this aspect of conditionals. So for present purposes, you should not be troubled by it either.

Conditionals are very important in most reasoning, so it is crucial that you become both familiar with and comfortable working with conditionals. But conditionals can be tricky, and we will now turn to three important complications raised by conditionals.

1.3.2.3.1 Translation   Let *A* stand for the antecedent and *C* for the consequent of a conditional. Each of the following is an expression of the conditional "If *A* then *C*:"

> *C* if *A*; given *A*, *C*; not *A* unless *C*; *A* implies *C*; *A* only if *C*; whenever *A*, *C*; *A* is a sufficient condition for *C*; *C* is a necessary condition for *A*

> ☀ **Caution**   *if* and *only if:* Normally the statement that follows *if* occupies the antecedent position of a conditional, and *the statement that follows the expression **only if** is always the consequent.* Thus, for example, the statement "Only if J. C. is found guilty will he go to prison" translates as "If J. C. goes to prison, then he has been found guilty." Try this with each of the other variations, letting *A* equal "J. C. goes to prison" and *C* equal "J. C. is found guilty," and note that each variation translates into one and the same conditional. Once again, be very careful about what is the antecedent and what is the consequent. The truth table for conditionals is very specific about when a conditional is false: the antecedent must be true and the consequent must be false. It is very important to determine correctly which is which.

1.3.2.3.2 Necessary and Sufficient Conditions   When we say that something *X* is sufficient for something else *Y,* what we mean is that the occurrence of *X* suffices to bring about *Y;* that is, if *X* occurs then *Y* also occurs. So when we say that *X* is sufficient for *Y,* we mean that *X* is the antecedent and *Y* is the consequent of the conditional "if X then Y." On the other hand, when we say that something W is necessary for something else Z, what we mean is that Z will not occur unless W occurs. That is, Z will occur only if W occurs. Given what we have said before, it should be obvious that *when we say that* W *is necessary for* Z, *we mean that* Z *is the antecedent and* W *is the consequent of the conditional "if* Z, *then* W."

> **Tip**   How do you show that something A is not necessary (or sufficient) for something else B? The answer should now be obvious: express the matter in terms of a conditional (making sure that you locate antecedent and consequent properly) and show that this conditional is false; that is, it has a true antecedent and a false consequent.

To Think About

What Is a Legal System?   What makes a legal system different from other types of phenomena that resemble it in some important ways (for example, religion). For the answer we must turn to a conditional analysis. To this effect, we might ask whether there are any *necessary* conditions for something's being a legal system; if so, then we would say that anything lacking that feature could not be a legal system. We might also ask whether there are any *sufficient* conditions, such that anything possessing those features would have to be a legal system. We could even inquire about whether there is anything *distinctive* about legal systems, in the sense that there is a feature or set of features that is *both necessary and sufficient* for legal systems, that is, it is found in legal systems and nothing else. There have been numerous attempts in the history of jurisprudence to answer these questions, which turn out to be more difficult than they might first seem. For instance, one might speculate that incorporation of a popularly elected legislature is a necessary condition, but the legal system of Vatican City has no such feature. Likewise, the presence of a police force might be thought to be a sufficient condition, but the presence of all sorts of "private police forces" seems at odds with that claim. And having a set of judges to make authoritative rulings is not distinctive to legal systems: umpires act as "judges" in baseball, and even the "Miss America Pageant" contest is authoritatively decided by a set of appropriate judges. What are your suggestions?

1.3.2.3.3 General Statements   It may not be readily apparent that general statements ("unjust laws are resented," "use a gun, go to prison," "criminals ought to get punished," and so on) can be viewed as conditional statements. Thus, for example, the sentence "unjust laws are resented" can be understood as saying that "if something X is an unjust law, then X is resented." The virtue of expressing the matter this way is that we can now clearly see what would be required in order to falsify this conditional statement: we need to find a case that shows us that the antecedent is true and yet the consequent is false. Thus if we find an unjust law that is not resented, the general statement we started with can be rejected as false.

1.3.2.4 Biconditionals

These compounds are also called *equivalences,* and they are formed with the expression "if and only if." Thus the statement

    1. J. C. is a criminal if and only if he committed a crime.

is a biconditional compound whose components are "J. C. is a criminal" and "J. C. committed a crime." Since biconditionals express equivalences, it should be obvious that they turn out to be true if the component parts have the same truth value (that is, they are both true, or they are both false), and they turn out to be false when the component parts differ in truth value. That is, the truth conditions for biconditionals are as follows:

> For any two statements *A* and *B*, the **biconditional** "*A* if and only if *B*" is true when both *A* and *B* have the *same* truth value.

Notice that the biconditional "*A* if and only if *B*" is the conjunction of two conditionals, namely, "if *A*, then *B*" and "only if *A*, then *B*." Recalling the discussion of necessary and sufficient conditions earlier in this section, it should come as no surprise that the expression "*A* is both necessary and sufficient for *B*" translates as equivalent to "*A* if and only if *B*."

1.3.2.5 Negations

Despite appearances, a negative statement (for example, "J. R. is not a murderer") is also a truth-functional compound, for the truth value of the negated statement depends on the truth value of the affirmative statement: if a statement *A* is true, then *not A* is false; and if *A* is false, then its negation *not A* is true. In our example, "J. R. is not a murderer" is true if "J. R. is a murderer" is false. Here are three important points to note concerning negations:

- The word *not* is not the only one used to express negations. We also express the negation of a statement by affixing to it the phrases *it is not the case that* and *it is false that.*
- Be careful about the order of the words *both* and *not:* the sentence "*X* and *Y* will not both be arrested" says something different from the sentence "Both *X* and *Y* will not be arrested." The first sentence says that the conjunction "*X* will be arrested *and Y* will be arrested" is false, while the second sentence says "It is false that *X* will be arrested" *and* "It is false that *Y* will be arrested."
- The negation of a disjunction is often formed with the expression "Neither . . . nor. . . ." But be careful about the expression "Neither . . . nor. . . ." The statement "Neither *X* nor *Y* will be arrested" says that "It is false that *X* will be arrested" *and* "It is false that *Y* will be arrested."

Summary of Truth Conditions for Compounds

In logic every statement is either true or false. Thus for any two statements *A* and *B*, there are, obviously enough, four possibilities as to their truth value: (i) both *A* and *B* are true; (ii) both *A* and *B* are false; (iii) *A* is true and *B* is false; and (iv) *A* is false and *B* is true. Where *T* and *F* represent "true" and "false" respectively, we can schematically present all the possible combinations of the truth values of *A* and *B* in the following *truth table:*

A	*B*
T	T
T	F
F	T
F	F

Given that much, we can capture in a summary truth table the truth conditions for all the compound statements we have discussed. The summary truth table will be as follows:

A	*B*	*A* and *B*	*A* or *B*	If *A* then *B*	*A* if and only if *B*
T	T	T	T	T	T
F	T	F	T	T	F
T	F	F	T	F	F
F	F	F	F	T	T

A Note on Complex Compounds

Compound statements can be combined to form longer, more complex compounds. But in order to assess the truth value of complex compounds, we first have to disambiguate them. Thus, just as in math, we employ parentheses, brackets, and braces as punctuation marks. For example, the complex compound "Either *A* and *B* or *C*" is an ambiguous statement. Once disambiguated, it may yield "Either (*A* and *B*) or *C*" or it may yield "Either *A* and (*B* or *C*)."

How are we to decide how to punctuate in each particular case? For example, how are we to disambiguate the statement:

1. If either J. C. is found guilty and he goes to prison, or Nick's murderer is captured, justice will be done.

Unfortunately, there is no universal, mechanical, or "blind" way of deciding. Each case must be dealt with individually. One has to pay attention to such things as commas and periods, the context of the sentence, and the overall "spirit" of what is conveyed. There is no substitute for being a careful, experienced speaker (and listener!) of the language. But if there is one essential piece of advice, it would be this: *go from the outside, as it were, and attempt to find the main connective first.* That is, look at the whole compound and decide *overall* what type of statement you think it is (is it a conditional, a disjunction, or what?) Once this has been determined, move on to the component parts, and if these are themselves compounds, repeat the process. For example, it seems that sentence 1 above is, overall, a conditional, namely:

> 1'. *If* (either J. C. is found guilty and he goes to prison, or Nick's murderer is captured), *then* justice will be done.

The antecedent of this conditional is also a compound. Given the placement of the comma, however, it seems that the antecedent is overall a disjunction whose one disjunct is a conjunction. Thus as a final result we have:

> 1". *If* [(J. C. is found guilty *and* he goes to prison) *or* (Nick's murderer is captured)], *then* justice will be done.

This relatively simple strategy can be applied to every case requiring disambiguation. However, do not be misled into believing that things are always easy or straightforward. Since there is no simple mechanical rule for translation, it is imperative to practice the technique of finding the main connective and "working inward" from there, and to try to develop a sensitivity to the nuances of language.

1.3.3 Relations of Statements

Statements stand in important logical relationships to each other. This is a major topic within logic, but you should be aware of at least the following relations.

Equivalences   *Two statements are equivalent if they have exactly the same truth value.* Here are some equivalences that are particularly useful:

1. "If *A* then *B*" is equivalent to "If not *B* then not *A*."
2. "If *A* then *B*" is equivalent to "Not *A* unless *B*."
3. "If *A* then *B*" is equivalent to "It is not the case that *A* and not *B*."

The truth of these equivalences should be obvious once we think in terms of necessary and sufficient conditions. Consider statement 1: the first statement in 1 says, in effect, that the occurrence of *B* is a necessary condition for *A* to occur. But this means that if *B* is not there, *A* is not going to be there either. And this is exactly what the second part of 1 says. Similarly with statement 2: read the first part of statement 2 in terms of necessary conditions. To say that *B* is necessary for

A, is to say that *A* is not going to occur unless we have *B.* And, again, this is what the second part of 2 says. Finally, read the first part of 3 in terms of sufficient conditions: it says that *A* suffices to bring about *B; A* by itself alone brings about *B.* But this in turn means that once *A* is present, then *B* "automatically" is coming about too. So how can it be that you can have *A* and not have *B?* You just cannot have *A* and not have *B* in this case. And this is what the second part of 3 says.

Contraposition and Conversion

💣 **Caution** The equivalence expressed in statement 1 above is called *contraposition.* Notice that, in general, to form the *contrapositive* of a conditional we first reverse the terms (that is, we turn the antecedent into a consequent and vice versa), and then we negate them both. But be very careful. Simply reversing the terms of a conditional (forming its *converse*) does not make the new conditional equivalent to the original: "If *x* is a dog, then *x* is an animal" is always true; but when we reverse the terms to form the converse statement "if *x* is an animal, then *x* is a dog," we no longer have an always true statement. More generally, it is a serious mistake to think that "if *A* then *B*" is equivalent to its converse "if *B* then *A.*"

Contradictions *Two statements are contradictory if they have exactly opposite truth values* (that is, when one is true the other *must* be false and vice versa). A moment's reflection will reveal that the following are contradictory:

1. Any statement *A* and its negation *not A.*
2. "All *S* are *P*" and "Some *S* are not *P.*"
3. "No *S* are *P*" and "Some *S* are *P.*"

Contraries *Two statements are contraries if they cannot both be true, yet they* **may** *both be false.* For example, the statements

1. J. C. is the single murderer of Helen.
2. J. R. is the single murderer of Helen.

cannot both be true (since, *ex hypothesi,* there is only one murderer), but they could both be false (it may be that the real murderer is some third person *X,* or that Helen was murdered by more than one person). Similarly the statements

3. *A* is a better lawyer than *B.*
4. *B* is a better lawyer than *A.*

cannot both be true, but they may both be false (*A* and *B* may well be equally good). Finally, the statements

5. All murderers get the death sentence.
6. No murderer gets the death sentence.

are contraries, since the truth may be that some murderers get the death sentence while other murderers receive lesser sentences.

Confusing Contraries and Contradictories

💣 **Caution**   Be very careful! One of the most common mistakes is to talk loosely of "opposites" and to miss the crucial difference between contradictory and contrary statements. Inattention to this difference can be easily exploited by those who present you with "false dilemmas," situations that present just two alternatives that are allegedly the only available ones in order to force you to choose one of them. Consider, for example, "we will either sentence him to death or we will let him go free." Why can't we do some third thing? We must always be alert to the fact that many pairs of "opposites" are actually in a relation of contrariety rather than contradiction (for example, day-night, smart-dumb, good-evil, tall-short), so that instead of choosing *between* them we can always go *through* them and opt for a third alternative.

TO THINK ABOUT

"An Unjust Law Is Not Law."   This is a statement that is attributed to the prominent advocate of *natural law* (see Appendix II), St. Thomas Aquinas. Use the equivalences discussed in section 1.3.3 to give alternative readings of this statement. Then answer the following questions:

- Does the statement imply that a just law is law? Why or why not?

- What does this statement imply about the role of justice for the status of (a) a particular *law* being a genuine law of a given legal system and (b) a particular *legal system* being a genuine legal system?

- Is there a way to read this statement as a *necessary proposition* (section 1.3.1.1)? If yes, how exactly? What could be the problem(s) of such a reading? If not, why do you think this is a *contingent proposition* (section 1.3.1.1)?

- What would be the "opposite" of this statement? What sort of "opposition" have we here?

TEST YOUR KNOWLEDGE #3

Answer "true" or "false." (If you get less than 90% correct, go back and reread. The answers are at the end of part I.)

_____ 1. A conjunction that has one false component is false.

_____ 2. A conjunction is true in just one case.

_____ 3. A disjunction that has one false component is false.

_____ 4. Where *A* and *B* are statements, the expression "*A* is a necessary condition for *B*" translates as "If *A* then *B*."

_____ 5. A conditional with false antecedent is always false.

_____ 6. A conditional with false consequent is always false.

_____ 7. Where *W* and *Z* are statements, the expression "not *Z* unless *W*" translates as "if *W*, then *Z*."

_____ 8. "We shall win if we fight" translates as "If we win, then we fight."

_____ 9. "We shall win only if we fight" translates as "If we fight, we shall win."

_____ 10. "We shall win if and only if we fight" translates as "If we fight, we shall win."

_____ 11. We argue that *A* is not necessary for *B* by showing that there is a case where *A* is true and yet *B* is false.

_____ 12. "Jurors are selected objectively" is a biconditional statement.

_____ 13. "Both *X* and *Y* will not be arrested" translates as "*X* will not be arrested and *Y* will not be arrested."

_____ 14. "Neither *A* nor *B*" translates as "not *A* and not *B*."

_____ 15. "*A* only if *B*" is equivalent to "If *B* then *A*."

_____ 16. The statements "No criminals get the death sentence" and "Some criminals get the death sentence" are contraries.

_____ 17. The statements "E.T.G. is the sole killer of Mary" and "R.F.G. is the sole killer of Mary" are contradictory.

_____ 18. "If *A* then *B*" is equivalent to "not *A* unless *B*."

_____ 19. "If *X* then *Y*" is equivalent to "If not *Y* then not *X*."

_____ 20. "Check box 1 only if either you are married and have children or you are a head of household" is an overall disjunctive compound.

CHAPTER 2

ARGUMENTS

2.1 THE NATURE OF ARGUING

Imagine the following exchange between persons *A* and *B*:

A: Capital punishment ought to be abolished.

B: O.k., I guess if you say so, it must be so.

What is wrong with this picture? If we focus on just what *A* said, the answer is "nothing, really." But if we focus on *B*'s reaction to what *A* said, then the answer is "everything that a rational person fears." Why so? Because although *A* sets forth a highly controversial claim and offers no reason whatsoever *why* we should believe it, *B* accepts it unquestionably and "on blind faith." *B*'s attitude is in effect a dismissal, a denial, of the argumentative process: there is no attempt of any sort to engage in rational scrutiny of this controversial claim.

Now imagine the following alternative scenario:

A: Capital punishment ought to be abolished.

C: Well, *why* is what you say true?

A: Because capital punishment does not deter people from committing crimes, and moreover it is a cruel and unusual punishment that is prohibited by the Constitution.

What we have here is a picture of the initiation of the argumentative process, a picture that is made possible when *C* adopts an inquisitive, almost confrontational, attitude toward *A*'s controversial claim and asks the crucial question, "*What reasons* can you provide for accepting that what you said is true?" In asking the "why so?" question, *C* has challenged *A* to provide some support, or justification, for his claim. And to the degree that *A* responds in the manner of "My claim is true because . . .", *A* is offering an *argument* for his position.

A few things should already be clear regarding what is *not* involved in the process of giving an argument: it is not to merely exchange points and counterpoints; it is not to raise your voice or insult someone; it is not to say with a strong tone that you insist on this, or that you strongly believe this; it is not to appeal to the emotions and/or goodwill of your audience.

What *is* involved in the argumentative process then? An initial answer might be "a proof of sorts; a dispassionate attempt to rationally convince that some claim *P* is indeed true." But this initial answer needs to be narrowed down somewhat. Proofs to the effect that *P* is true can take many forms: you can present the facts that provide evidence for it, conduct experiments that confirm it, show pictures, and so on. But the sort of justification that is involved in *argumentative* proofs is quite specific: we demonstrate the truth of some problematic claim *P by means of other claims* that are purportedly unproblematic; the truth of *P* is supposed to be inferred from (to follow from) the purported truth of the claims that are advanced in its support. In other words, the justification involved in argumentation is logical or inferential; one claim is logically derived from other claims. Let us now turn specifically to the logician's notion of argument.

2.2 Arguments in Logic and Arguments in Ordinary Discourse

In any standard logic book, the term *argument* will be defined along the following lines:

> **Argument**   A group of statements some of which, called the *premises,* purport to provide support for the truth of a controversial statement called the *conclusion.*

Logicians refer to the process by which we derive a conclusion from a set of premises as *inference*. Putting aside some complications, in the present context we will be using the terms *argument* and *inference* interchangeably. Following are a few crucial points to note based on the logician's definition of *argument*.

Not every group of statements is an argument: Arguments have an internal structure and assert that there is a logical link between the statements in the group. The conclusion is purportedly implied by (is inferred from, follows from) the premises.

In the simplest case, an argument requires at least two statements: (i) a conclusion—a claim that is controversial enough to need justification, and (ii) a premise—a claim that is (purportedly) uncontroversial, and which is offered as a supporting reason for the truth of the conclusion. Of course, arguments typically involve several premises.

Incomplete arguments (enthymemes): The basic formal pattern of an argument is roughly this:

Premise 1

Premise 2

:

Premise *n*

_____

Conclusion

In ordinary discourse, however, arguments often appear to be missing some premises or even a conclusion. Likewise, the order of statements is not always that the premises appear first and the conclusion last. For example, in

J. R. should be in prison, since he murdered his wife.

the conclusion comes first, and there is a missing premise that might be articulated as "Murderers should be in prison." Arguments that have missing parts, premises, or conclusions that are not explicitly stated are called *enthymemes.* Arguments are sometimes (but not always) expressed in this "abbreviated" way because the speaker believes that the missing part is so obvious that the audience will readily supply it on their own.

The terms *premise* and *conclusion* are relative: Since arguments come in chains, one and the same statement might be a premise in one argument and the conclusion of another, and vice versa.

Consider the following arguments:

(1) All authors of Supreme Court opinions are justices of the Court.

(2) Clarence Thomas is the author of Supreme Court opinions.

(3) Thus, Clarence Thomas is a justice of the Supreme Court.

and

(1) If one is a Supreme Court justice, one has been confirmed by the Senate.

(2) Clarence Thomas is a Supreme Court justice.

(3) Thus, Clarence Thomas was confirmed by the Senate.

In the first argument, "Clarence Thomas is a Supreme Court justice" is the conclusion of the argument, whereas in the second argument the statement serves as the second premise.

This phenomenon can occur within one single argumentative chain, as in this example:

(1) People who get away with murder should be punished.

(2) J. R. got away with murder.

(3) Thus, J. R. should be punished.

(4) If J. R. should be punished, J. R. should go to prison.

(5) Thus, J. R. should go to prison.

Here (3) is derived from (1) and (2) as the conclusion of an argument, but it is also a premise for a second argument that uses (3) in combination with (4) and concludes with (5).

Arguments are not explanations: Although both arguments and explanations have the form "Claim *P* is true because . . . ," there is a difference between the two. We give an argument in order to convince the audience that some controversial claim *P* is true. If the audience already believes that *P* is true, there is literally no point in arguing for the truth of *P.* On the other hand, we do offer explanations for what we (and our audience) take to be true. We can explain, that is, *why* some uncontroversial claim *P* is the case. Thus, for example, we *argue* for the truth of the controversial claim, "The Republicans will lose the 2000 presidential election," but we *explain* why "The Republicans lost the 1996 presidential election" is true.

> **Tip**   Notice that the preceding remarks suggest an important practical implication about argumentation: in presenting an argument for claim *P,* since *P* is controversial, always keep in mind that there are people who do not believe that *P* is true. But these people are precisely the audience to whom you need to address your argument—you need to convince the unconvinced. And that can involve quite a struggle.

Distinguishing premises and conclusions is not a mechanical task: In analyzing and assessing arguments in ordinary language, the first (and arguably most crucial) step is to distinguish the argument's premises from its conclusion(s). Fortunately, argumentative passages frequently contain clues—called *indicator words*—that signal whether we are confronted with a premise or a conclusion. Here is a partial list of some common indicators:

> **Conclusion Indicators:** therefore; hence; thus; so; consequently; it follows that; accordingly; in conclusion; whence; as a result; we may infer that; for this reason; it is implied that; it is entailed that.

> **Premise Indicators:** since; because; for; as; given that; inasmuch as; follows from; may be by; for the reason that; in view of the fact that.

These indicators are usually very reliable in identifying premises and conclusions. But this does not mean that the process of identification is "mechanical." One problem is that indicators are sometimes missing. Consider, for example, the following argument:

> We need to build more prisons in order to cope with the continuous increase in crime. In view of the currently overcrowded prison conditions, many criminals are confined in prison for a much lesser time than they should be. But it is

common knowledge that criminals tend to repeat their crimes when they are out of prison.

Notice that neither conclusion indicators nor premise indicators appear in this passage. Yet it looks very much like an argument. *But how does one determine which claims are premises and which is the conclusion?* One helpful strategy is the following:

> **Outline Method for Analyzing Arguments** Begin by trying to locate the passage's overall conclusion. To do this, you need to ask the crucial question: *Just what is the point the author is trying to make?* Having answered this question, and having successfully identified the conclusion, you can then go on to ask: *In what way(s) is this conclusion supported?* The answer(s) to this latter question ought to yield the premises.

This is hardly a foolproof method, but in analyzing passages containing no premise or conclusion indicators, asking the questions we have suggested in the order we have suggested, while paying careful attention to the context, should be enough to accomplish the task most of the time. (As a test, apply this simple technique to the preceding argument that lacks indicator words and see whether it yields, as it should, the first sentence as the conclusion, and the rest as the premises.)

Main arguments and subarguments: Actual argumentative passages can be complicated. Part of the complexity arises when authors recognize that one or more of the claims they make in the course of their overall argument are not as uncontroversial as they would like. To deal with this, authors undertake the additional task of providing subarguments in support of the most controversial premises of their main argument. *How does one deal with complex passages containing subarguments in support of the claims of the main argument?* Although there is no mechanical formula for analyzing these passages, a "backwards strategy" (one that resembles the method we have seen in section 1.3.2 for disambiguating compound statements—find the main connective and work inward from there) may be the following:

> **Outline Method for Reading Complex Argumentative Passages** Attempt to pinpoint the final, main conclusion of the overall argument and *work backward* from there to identify the main premises of the overall argument. (Hint: they are usually controversial themselves.) When this is finished, repeat the process for the subarguments. If despite conscientious efforts you still fail, it may not be your fault; it may well be that the author of the argument has been inattentive, or simply confused and confusing.

PRACTICE MAKES PERFECT

Make your best effort to identify and analyze the arguments in the following passages.

> The States' primary claim is that death is a necessary punishment because it prevents the commission of capital crimes more effectively than any less severe punishment. The first part of this claim is that the infliction of death is necessary to stop the individuals executed from committing further crimes. The sufficient answer to this is that if a criminal convicted of a capital crime poses a danger to society, effective administration of the State's pardon and parole laws can delay or deny his release from prison, and techniques of isolation can eliminate or minimize the danger while he remains confined. The more significant argument is that the threat of death prevents the commission of capital crimes because it deters potential criminals who would not be deterred by the threat of imprisonment. The argument is not based upon evidence that the threat of death is a superior deterrent. Indeed, as my Brother Marshall establishes, the available evidence uniformly indicates, although it does not conclusively prove, that the threat of death has no greater deterrent effect than the threat of imprisonment.
>
> From Justice Brennan's opinion in *Furman v. Georgia,* 408 U.S. (1972)

> If the Georgia statute cannot be enforced as it is written—if the conduct it seeks to prohibit is a protected form of liberty for the vast majority of Georgia's citizens—the State must assume the burden of justifying a selective application of its law. Either the persons to whom Georgia seeks to apply its statute do not have the same interest in "liberty" that others have, or there must be a reason why the State may be permitted to apply a generally applicable law to certain persons that it does not apply to others. The first possibility is plainly unacceptable. Although the meaning of the principle that "all men are created equal" is not always clear, it surely must mean that every free citizen has the same interest in "liberty" that the members of the majority share. . . . The second possibility is similarly unacceptable. A policy of selective application must be supported by a neutral and legitimate interest—something more substantial than a habitual dislike for, or ignorance about, the disfavored group. Neither the State nor the Court has identified any such interest in this case.
>
> From Justice Stevens's dissent in *Bowers v. Hardwick,* 487 U.S. 186 (1986)

> Today, education is perhaps the most important function of state and local governments. Compulsory school attendance laws and the great expenditures for education both demonstrate our recognition of the importance of education to our democratic society. It is required in the performance of our most basic public responsibilities, even service in the armed forces. It is the very foundation of good citizenship. Today it is a principal instrument in awakening the child to cultural values, in preparing him for later professional training, and in helping him to adjust normally to his environment. In these days, it is

doubtful that any child may reasonably be expected to succeed in life if he is denied the opportunity of an education. Such an opportunity, where the state has undertaken to provide it, is a right which must be made available to all on equal terms.

From Justice Warren's opinion in Brown v. Board of Education,
347 U.S. 483 (1954)

Now in human societies the death penalty has been laid down for many offences less serious than this one. Yet people still take risks when they feel sufficiently confident. No one has ever yet risked committing a crime which he thought he could not carry out successfully. The same is true of states. None has yet rebelled in the belief that it had insufficient resources, either in itself or from its allies, to make the attempt. Cities and individuals alike, are by nature disposed to do wrong, and there is no law that will prevent it, as it is shown by the fact that men have tried every kind of punishment, constantly adding to the list, in the attempt to find greater security from criminals. It is likely that in early times the punishments even for the greatest crimes were not as severe as they are now, but the laws were still broken, and in the course of time the death penalty became generally introduced. Yet even with this, the laws are still broken. Either, therefore, we must discover some fear more potent than the fear of death, or we must admit that here certainly we have not got an adequate deterrent. So long as poverty forces men to be bold, so long as the insolence and pride of wealth nourishes their ambitions, and in the other accidents of life they are continually dominated by some incurable master passion or another, so long will their impulses continue to drive them into danger. Hope and desire persist throughout and cause the greatest calamities—one leading and the other following, one conceiving the enterprise, and the other suggesting that it will be successful—invisible factors, but more powerful than the terrors that are obvious to the eye. Then too, the idea that fortune will be on one's side plays as big a part as anything else in creating a mood of overconfidence. . . . In a word it is impossible (and only the most simple-minded will deny this) for human nature, when once seriously set upon a certain course, to be prevented from following that course by the force of law or by any other means of intimidation whatever. We must not, therefore, come to the wrong conclusions through having too much confidence in the effectiveness of capital punishment. . . .

From Thucydides, The Peloponnesian War, Bk. 3, 43–46

The third reason [that has been advanced to justify anti-abortion laws] is the State's interest—some phrase it in terms of duty—in protecting prenatal life. Some of the argument for this justification rests on the theory that a new human life is present from the moment of conception. . . .

The appellee and certain amici argue that the fetus is a "person" within the language and meaning of the Fourteenth Amendment. In support of this they outline at length and in detail the well-known facts of fetal development. If this suggestion of personhood is established, the appellant's case, of course, collapses, for the fetus' right to life is then guaranteed specifically by the Amendment. The appellant conceded as much on reargument. On the other hand, the appellee conceded on reargument that no case could be cited that holds that a fetus is a person within the meaning of the Fourteenth Amendment.

All this, together with our observation, *supra,* that throughout the major portion of the 19th century prevailing legal abortion practices were far freer than they are today, persuades us that the word "person," as used in the Fourteenth Amendment, does not include the unborn. . . . Indeed, our decision in *United States v. Vuitch,* 402 U.S. 62 (1971), inferentially is to the same effect, for we would not have indulged in statutory interpretation favorable to abortion in specified circumstances if the necessary consequence was the termination of life entitled to Fourteenth Amendment protection. . . .

We need not resolve the difficult question of when life begins. When those trained in the respective disciplines of medicine, philosophy, and theology are unable to arrive at any consensus, the judiciary, at this point in the development of man's knowledge, is not in a position to speculate as to the answer.

It should be sufficient to note briefly the wide divergence of thinking on this most sensitive and difficult question. There has always been strong support for the view that life does not begin until live birth. This was the belief to the Stoics. It appears to be the predominant, though not the unanimous, attitude of the Jewish faith. It may be taken to represent also the position of a large segment of the Protestant community, insofar as that can be ascertained; organized groups that have taken a formal position on the abortion issue have generally regarded abortion as a matter for the conscience of the individual and her family. As we have noted, the common law found greater significance in quickening. Physicians and their scientific colleagues have regarded that event with less interest and have tended to focus either upon conception or upon live birth or upon the interim point at which the fetus becomes "viable," that is, potentially able to live outside the mother's womb, albeit with artificial aid. Viability is usually placed at about seven months (28 weeks) but may occur earlier, even at 24 weeks. . . .

In areas other than criminal abortion the law has been reluctant to endorse any theory that life, as we recognize it, begins before live birth or to accord legal rights to the unborn except in narrowly defined situations and except when the rights are contingent upon live birth. . . . In short, the unborn have never been recognized in the law as persons in the whole sense.

In view of all this, we do not agree that, by adopting one theory of life, Texas may override the rights of the pregnant woman that are at stake. . . .

From Justice Harry A. Blackmun's majority opinion in *Roe v. Wade,*
410 U.S. 113 (1973)

2.3 KINDS OF ARGUMENT: DEDUCTIVE VERSUS INDUCTIVE REASONING

Logicians traditionally divide reasoning into two major categories: deductive and inductive. The difference between these two types of reasoning is characterized in a variety of ways, and in what follows we discuss two of those ways that we believe are most useful.

2.3.1 The First Distinction: Necessity versus Probability

One way to draw the distinction between deductive and inductive arguments is in terms of the strength of the logical link between premises and conclusion as follows:

> In a "good" deductive argument, the truth of the premises *necessitates* the truth of the conclusion. In a "good" inductive argument, by contrast, the truth of the premises merely makes the conclusion *probable*.

Two widely used "textbook examples" illustrate this point:

A. All men are mortal, and Socrates is a man. Thus, Socrates is mortal.

B. The sun has risen every morning to this day. Thus, probably, the sun will also rise tomorrow.

Argument A is a deductive argument. Intuitively, at this point, we can see that this argument is a "good" one, at least in the sense that the conclusion seems to "follow" from the premises. Now it may be that we discover that Socrates is a Martian life-form, and thus it may turn out that not all of the premises of A are actually true. Nonetheless, if we *assume* that the premises of A *are* indeed true, then the conclusion (that he is mortal) would be absolutely certain, or *necessarily true*.

Argument B is an inductive argument. Intuitively, it is also a "good" one; the premise is indeed true, and seems to provide excellent evidential support for the truth of the conclusion. But notice that while the premise states a claim about our past experience, the conclusion "goes beyond" the premise and projects from this past experience to a future case. But then the truth of the premise cannot conclusively guarantee the truth of the conclusion. There is a possibility, however slim, that the laws of nature will fail us tomorrow morning and the sun will not rise. Hence, the truth of the premises renders the conclusion only *probably true*.

2.3.2 The Second Distinction: Criteria of Appraisal

We have used the term *good* as an initial, intuitive notion for evaluating arguments. But we can attain more precision in distinguishing deductive and inductive arguments by adopting the criteria of appraisal developed by logicians:

> Deductive arguments are appraised as being either *valid* or *invalid*. Inductive arguments, by contrast, are given a position in a continuum of strength that has very *weak* or worthless arguments at the low end and extremely *strong* arguments at the apex.

In what follows we discuss briefly the basic issues involved in appraising deductive and inductive arguments.

2.3.2.1 Appraisal of Deductive Arguments

Two key notions are used to evaluate deductive arguments, namely, *validity* and *soundness.* The main points to remember regarding each of these notions are as follows.

    Validity   Validity is the most central notion of deductive logic. Unfortunately, it is also the notion that is most commonly misunderstood by the beginning student. Validity concerns the logical relationship between premises and conclusion. Roughly, it is a matter of whether or not the conclusion of a deductive argument follows (logically) from its premises. A bit more precisely,

> A **valid** deductive argument is one that, *on the assumption* that the premises are true, has a true conclusion that follows with necessity from the premises.

That is, if we *cannot* imagine, conceive, speculate, or think the conclusion to be false at the same time we hypothesize that the premises are true, then the argument is valid. If we *can* imagine the conclusion to be false while the premises are thought to be true, the argument is invalid. We can formulate this point as an intuitive test for validity as follows:

> **Practical Test of Validity**   Can one simultaneously think that the premises are true and that the conclusion is false? If the answer is "yes," the argument is invalid. If the answer is "no," the argument is valid.

    💣 **Caution**   It is very important to realize that, as far as validity goes, we do not need to know beforehand that the premises are *in fact* true, and we do not bother to make sure that they are in fact true either. Whether an argument is (or is not) valid has nothing to do with whether the premises are (or are not) *in fact* true. That is, the key point to remember is that the practical assessment of validity involves a two-step process. As a first step, we *suppose* that the premises are true; and as a second step, we ask ourselves whether we can now think of circumstances under which the conclusion is false. Thus, the assessment of the *actual* truth of the premises is not necessary as far as validity goes. Indeed, a deductive argument may have in fact false premises, or even false premises and a false conclusion, and still be valid. Conversely, a deductive argument may have obviously true premises and still be invalid. When we discussed the argument about Socrates's mortality earlier, we hinted at this. But since the connection between truth and validity is the source of common confusion, some additional examples may help to make this point clear.

Case 1 (valid, yet dubiously true premises): During the O. J. Simpson trial, defense attorneys pointed to a bloody glove that the murderer allegedly wore while committing the crime and offered the following argument:

If the glove does not fit, you must acquit.

The glove does not fit (O. J. Simpson).

Therefore, you must acquit (O. J. Simpson).

Is this a good argument as far as validity goes? A moment's reflection will reveal that it is. Never mind whether the premises are actually true. The argument is valid irrespective of the actual truth or falsity of the claims contained within it. For the issue of the validity of this (and every) argument is only the issue of *whether the conclusion could be thought of as false at the same time we suppose the premises to be true.* Again, a moment's reflection shows that this cannot be done in this case: to suppose the conclusion to be false, we need to suppose that at least one of the premises is not true. That is, if we suppose that we must not acquit O. J. Simpson, then either (a) the glove does not fit, or (b) even if the glove does fit, that does not mean we have to acquit. By contrast, consider the next case.

Case 2 (invalid, yet true premises): Suppose that the following argument is presented to someone who has never heard of the "trial of the century":

If O. J.'s attorneys had used a compelling defense, O. J. would have been acquitted.

O.J. has been acquitted.

Therefore, O. J.'s attorneys had used a compelling defense.

The second premise is true (O. J. Simpson was in fact acquitted), and suppose for present purposes that the first premise is also true. Nonetheless, the conclusion may be false. Notice that when we say that the conclusion may be false, this is not because we *know* it to be in fact false, but because we can *imagine* it to be false at the same time that we have supposed the premises to be true. We can hypothesize a variety of scenarios in which Simpson was acquitted, yet his attorneys presented a terrible, inept defense. How so? Perhaps the jury was swayed by sympathy for his children; or perhaps the prosecution's case was even more inept than that of the defense, or the prosecution's key witnesses were not credible; or perhaps it was O. J.'s conduct at the trial (rather than his attorney's arguments) that caused the jury to acquit. In each of these scenarios, the premises remain true—O. J. was acquitted, as he would have been *if* his attorneys had presented a compelling defense (but in these scenarios, he was acquitted *despite* his attorneys' ineptitude). So we can consistently imagine circumstances that would make the premises true and the conclusion false. This is sufficient to show that the argument is invalid.

Soundness If the actual truth (or falsity) of an argument's premises and conclusion is not important in determining validity, does it have any role to play in the evaluation of the argument? The answer is "yes": to assess validity we *hypothesize* the truth of the premises. Suppose we find the argument to be valid.

The question that arises at this point is whether the premises are *indeed true*. If the answer is "yes," then the argument is not only valid, but *sound* as well. In short,

> A **sound** deductive argument is one that is (a) valid, and (b) has actually true premises.

If an argument is sound, its conclusion must be true. So clearly, a sound deductive argument is as "good" as an argument can be. However, whether the premises of a valid argument are actually true (whether the argument is also sound) is almost always a major point of contention. But we should emphasize that the issue of soundness requires consideration not only of the logical structure of the argument (in particular whether, if taken together, the premises imply the conclusion), but also of the *content* of those premises, that is, whether what the premises assert is actually true. This latter issue is not the domain of logic alone.

2.3.2.2 Appraisal of Inductive Arguments

Neither validity nor invalidity are used to appraise inductive arguments. In fact, since all inductive arguments "leave room" for the conclusion to be false (in the sense that they assert merely that the conclusion is *probably* true), they can be classified as deductively invalid. The crucial notion for appraising inductive arguments is *strength*. Inductive arguments range from very weak to very strong, depending on the evidential support that the premises provide for the conclusion. Inductive strength is a matter of degree, and (once again) there are no clear-cut mechanical rules for determining the exact degree of strength of a particular inductive argument. Consider, for example, the following inductive inference:

(1) The victim was murdered at her home with a knife belonging to her ex-husband.

(2) Blood found on the murder weapon matches that of the ex-husband.

(3) There is evidence that there was a violent fight between the victim and the murderer right before the murder, and the ex-husband has a history of violence toward his ex-wife.

(4) Three witnesses testified that they saw the victim's ex-husband's car parked outside the victim's home at the estimated time of death.

Therefore, probably, the ex-husband is the murderer.

Suppose that each of the premises of this inference is indeed true. Still, the premises do not provide conclusive reasons for believing the conclusion. At best, the evidential support the premises provide for the conclusion is strong enough for us to infer that the falsity of the conclusion is highly unlikely. Unlike the appraisal of deductive arguments, in which the argument remains valid regardless of any additional claims appended to the premises, the appraisal of inductive arguments involves additional complexity, since inductive inferences gain or lose strength when additional (relevant) information is added to the premises. For example, suppose we added to the preceding argument the premise,

(5) The ex-husband confessed to the crime.

This additional information significantly strengthens the probability of the conclusion. Yet suppose we also add the premise,

(6) Ten witnesses testified that the ex-husband was with them (and not at the victim's home) at the time of the murder.

Clearly, even though we may still believe that premises (1) through (5) are true, the addition of the information in (6) weakens the argument considerably. In this way, the strength of inductive inferences is sensitive to the strength of the evidence (both its quality and quantity) offered in support of its conclusion.

2.4 DEDUCTIVE REASONING AND METHODS OF APPRAISING VALIDITY

Logicians use several methods to appraise the validity of arguments. A detailed examination of these methods would not serve our purposes very well. Instead, it will be sufficient to alert you to three "quasi-practical" methods that can be readily mastered and used by the nonexpert logician. In the text that follows we discuss these methods.

2.4.1 The First Method: The Practical Test of Validity

In section 2.3.2.1, we introduced a very simple and intuitive method for appraising the validity of a deductive argument, namely, *the practical test of validity.* For any simple (deductive) argument, we can always determine quickly whether it is invalid by performing this simple test. We mention this method here since it is, despite its limitations, one legitimate way to test for validity. And it is a limited method indeed: it is not always easy to produce scenarios that show the conclusion to be false despite the (hypothesized) truth of the premises. Yet for all our efforts the argument may still be invalid. Fortunately for us there are alternative (and less limited) methods we can employ.

2.4.2 The Second Method: Validity as a Matter of Form

Consider the following two arguments:

If you are innocent, you will be acquitted.

You are innocent.

Therefore, you will be acquitted.

You break the law, you go to jail.

You broke the law.

Therefore, you will go to jail.

Exactly what do these arguments have in common? Insofar as their subject matter differs, these are clearly two unrelated arguments. But if we focus on the way the premises and conclusions of both arguments are arranged, we then see that (i) each argument starts with a simple conditional statement, (ii) each continues by affirming the antecedent of its respective conditional, and (iii) each concludes by affirming the consequent of its respective conditional. But then these two obviously different arguments do seem to have something in common, namely, something *structural*—a common *pattern* or *form*. More explicitly, the "skeleton" for each of these arguments seems to be identical. Each follows this pattern:

If □ then O

□

Therefore O

Where the arguments differ is in how the square and the circle are filled respectively by each of them.

In the first argument, the square is filled by "you are innocent" and the circle by "you will be acquitted." In the second argument, the content of the square is "you broke the law," and the content of the circle is "you will go to jail." In each case, nonetheless, the pattern or form of argumentation is the same. Indeed both arguments can be said to be *substitution instances* of this same form. Can we take advantage of this fact in order to determine the validity of these arguments?

The answer is an unqualified "yes." Many arguments fall into groups that exhibit a certain structural pattern, a pattern that generations of students of logic have conclusively established as either valid or invalid. Knowledge of these patterns provides an easy, "blind" method for determining the validity or invalidity of a specific argument: if an argument is a substitution instance of a valid pattern, then it is itself a valid argument by virtue of having that valid pattern. Similarly, if an argument is a substitution instance of an invalid pattern, then the argument is invalid precisely because it exhibits that invalid pattern.

Just which patterns are valid or invalid? Our present goals would not be well served if we were to present as many of these patterns as we could find (there might be an infinite number of invalid argument forms!). Instead, we will limit our discussion to those that you are most likely to encounter. Our experience has shown that familiarity with these patterns is sufficient to enable those with no formal training in logic to deal with some of the most complex argumentative material.

2.4.2.1 Common Valid Patterns of Deductive Inference

Let the diagrams □, O, Δ, or alternatively, the letters *p, q, r,* stand for any simple or complex statement. Let ¬ stand for "it is not the case that," and let → stand for "if . . . then . . . ." The following patterns of deductive inference are always valid, and any concrete substitution instance of these patterns will always be a valid argument.

Modus Ponens **From a conditional and its antecedent, you can infer the consequent.**

PATTERN	SCHEMA	EXAMPLE
$\Box \rightarrow O$	if p then q	If a law is unjust, it is not law at all.
$\Box$	p	Euthanasia laws are unjust.
$\therefore O$	$\therefore q$	$\therefore$ Euthanasia laws are not laws at all.

Modus Tollens **From a conditional and the negation of its consequent, you can infer the negation of the antecedent.**

PATTERN	SCHEMA	EXAMPLE
$\Box \rightarrow O$	if p then q	If he was the murderer, he would be found guilty.
$\neg\, O$	*not q*	He was *not* found guilty.
$\therefore \neg\, \Box$	$\therefore$ *not p*	$\therefore$ He was *not* the murderer.

Hypothetical Syllogism **From two conditionals which are such that the consequent of one is the antecedent of the other, you can infer a third conditional formed out of the noncommon parts of the first two.**

PATTERN	SCHEMA	EXAMPLE
$\Box \rightarrow O$	if p then q	If J. C. is innocent, then J. C. will be acquitted.
$O \rightarrow \Delta$	if q then r	If J. C. is acquitted, then J. C. will be a free man.
$\therefore \Box \rightarrow \Delta$	$\therefore$ if p then r	$\therefore$ If J. C. is innocent, then J. C. will be a free man.

Disjunctive Syllogism **From a disjunction and the negation of one of the disjuncts, you can infer the other disjunct.**

PATTERN	SCHEMA	EXAMPLE
$\Box$ or O	p or q	Either J. R. is the murderer or J. C. is the murderer.
$\neg\, \Box$	*not p*	J. R. is *not* the murderer.
$\therefore O$	$\therefore q$	$\therefore$ J. C. is the murderer.

♠ **Caution**   Although the following points should be obvious from a careful reading of the valid inference patterns formulated in the preceding text, our experience shows that they cannot be overemphasized:

- *It does not matter in which order the premises appear.* For example, the following is also an instance of *modus tollens*, even though the statement that denies the consequent of the conditional appears first:

not q

if *p* then *q*

———————

∴ *not p*

- *It does not matter whether we are working with affirmative or with negative statements.* For example, the following are all valid *modus ponens* inferences:

If *not p*, then *not q*	If *not p*, then *q*	If *p*, then *not q*
not p	*not p*	*p*
∴ *not q*	∴ *q*	∴ *not q*

- *It does not matter whether we are working with simple or complex statements.* For example, the following is still a valid *disjunctive syllogism:*

    The jury found for the plaintiff and compensation was awarded, or the defendant won.

    It is not the case that the defendant won.

    ———————————————————————————

    ∴ The jury found for the plaintiff and compensation was awarded.

In this disjunctive syllogism, *p* is the compound statement "the jury found for the plaintiff and compensation was awarded," and *q* is "the defendant won." Notice that this example also shows that it does not matter *which* disjunct is negated in the process of a *disjunctive syllogism.*

- *Each of these patterns is valid because there is no way we can hypothesize the conclusion to be false while we simultaneously hypothesize the premises to be true.* Consider, for example, the *modus ponens* pattern shown earlier. To show it to be invalid, we would need to hypothesize that the conclusion is false while all the premises are true. Thus, for O (that is, the conclusion), we must assign "false." But then, in order for the premise □ → O to be true, □ (that is, the antecedent) must be assigned "false." (Since this premise is a conditional whose consequent is already assumed to be false, if the antecedent □ was assigned "true," then the whole conditional would be false.) But this means that now the second premise (that is, □) must be false. Thus, we cannot make all the premises true and the conclusion false. This inference cannot be invalid.

Notice that it does not matter where you begin. Start anywhere you wish, and remember to be consistent in your assignment of truth values. A good test of your understanding of validity and of what makes conditionals and disjunctions false would be to try your own proofs of the impossibility of invalidity for the remaining valid patterns.

2.4.2.2 Three Common *Invalid* Patterns

The following patterns of inference, common as they may be, are clearly invalid and should not be confused with the valid patterns of the previous section. It will be a good test of your understanding of validity to apply the practical test of validity to these patterns and verify their invalidity for yourself.

Denying the Antecedent   This pattern is a "corruption" of the *modus ponens* inference.

PATTERN	SCHEMA	EXAMPLE
$\square \rightarrow O$	if *p* then *q*	If you use a gun illegally, you go to jail.
$\neg \square$	*not p*	You did not use a gun illegally.
$\therefore \neg O$	$\therefore$ *not q*	$\therefore$ You will not go to jail.

Affirming the Consequent   This pattern is a "corruption" of the *modus tollens* inference.

PATTERN	SCHEMA	EXAMPLE
$\square \rightarrow O$	if *p* then *q*	If he was the murderer, he would be found guilty.
O	*q*	He was found guilty.
$\therefore \square$	$\therefore$ *p*	$\therefore$ He was the murderer.

Invalid Hypothetical Syllogism   This pattern is a "corruption" of the *hypothetical syllogism.*

PATTERN	SCHEMA	EXAMPLE
$\square \rightarrow O$	if *p* then *q*	If you are a police officer, you serve the law.
$O \rightarrow \triangle$	if *r* then *q*	If you are a judge, you serve the law.
$\therefore \square \rightarrow \triangle$	$\therefore$ if *p* then *r*	$\therefore$ If you are a police officer, you are a judge.

PRACTICE MAKES PERFECT

Identify the valid and invalid patterns of inference in the following *enthymemes* (see section 2.2).

1. He was not arrested, since he was innocent.

2. I do not know whether he is guilty, and if I do not know whether he is guilty, I cannot sentence him to prison.

3. Since J. R. did not murder anyone, it must be J. J. who is the murderer.

4. Had you used a gun to kill your victims, you would have ended up in jail. Thank God you used a knife.

5. If you are a criminal sentenced to life imprisonment, you spend your life in prison. But if you work all your life as a prison guard, you also spend your life in prison. Draw your own conclusions!

6. If people were afraid of the death penalty, they would not commit capital crimes. But people commit capital crimes all the time.

7. J. R. is not a criminal, since he did not kill J. J.

8. My client is either guilty or innocent, and he is not guilty.

9. My client could not have killed O. J.; at the time O. J. was stabbed to death in his New York apartment, my client was seen skiing in Colorado.

10. If you do not try, you cannot win. And you did not even try.

2.4.3 The Third Method: Showing Invalidity by Analogical Counterexample

The fact that questions of validity and invalidity can often be settled by focusing on the form of an argument suggests a third approach to assessing validity, an approach that focuses on the attempt to demonstrate the *invalidity* of a given argument form. We will begin by considering a version of a well-known philosophical discussion.

Consider someone who argues that probably *all* cases of type *A* have a characteristic *C,* given that *some* (or many, or most) cases of type *A* have characteristic *C.* For instance, suppose that we are presented with the following argument:

ARGUMENT *A*

Some judges are incompetent.

Thus, probably, all judges are incompetent.

Intuitively, we should suspect that there is something wrong with any attempt to draw a general conclusion on the basis of a partial sample. Nonetheless, how do we *prove* that this argument is invalid? Here is one way.

As a first step, we extract the form (pattern) of argument *A,* which seems to be something like this:

PATTERN *P*

Some *A*s are *B*s.

Thus, probably all *A*s are *B*s.

As a second step, we "fill in" this form with argumentative content that yields a patently invalid argument. In other words, we construct an argument *B* that shares with argument *A* pattern *P,* and yet argument *B* is clearly and obviously an invalid argument. For example, one argument that would fit this bill is,

ARGUMENT *B*

Some paintings are forgeries.

Thus, probably, all paintings are forgeries.

Argument *B* is obviously invalid, since it has a clearly true premise and a blatantly false conclusion. (For how can it be that *all* paintings are forgeries? If that were possible, then there would not be any originals. But in the absence of any originals, how could there be any forgeries?)

Finally, we argue that since argument pattern *P* has a clearly invalid substitution instance (argument *B*), pattern *P* is invalid. Since argument *A* is a substitution instance of a pattern that we now (in view of *B*) know to be invalid, argument *A* must also be invalid.

> ✎ **Note**   Successfully applying this method requires some ingenuity, since there are no hard-and-fast rules for producing examples that: (a) duplicate the structure of the original argument, yet (b) are clearly and obviously invalid. Moreover, we must again emphasize that this method works only for proving the *invalidity* of an argument.

2.4.4 Two Trouble Spots for Validity: Equivocation and Circular Arguments

Beware of two potential pitfalls in appraising the validity of deductive arguments: (i) arguments that commit the fallacy of equivocation, and (ii) arguments that beg the question (circular arguments). We examine these arguments in the following text.

2.4.4.1 Apparently Valid but It Is Not: Equivocation
In the discussion of language in chapter 1, we pointed out that one and the same term may have multiple meanings. Although there is nothing wrong with words having multiple meanings, difficulties arise when (whether intentionally or unintentionally) we shift meanings in the course of an argument. For example, consider the following argument:

> All laws are subject to interpretation by the judiciary.
>
> The Pareto Principle is a law of economics.
>
> Therefore, the Pareto Principle is subject to interpretation by the judiciary.

Although this argument seems to be valid (it appears to be an instance of the valid modus ponens form), it also seems to have rather obviously true premises and a false conclusion (which is a clear sign of invalidity). What has gone wrong? The answer is that we have *equivocated* in our use of the term *law*. Clearly the laws mentioned in the first premise are statutory laws, while the second premise is about the laws of economics. We shifted meanings for the term *law*, and the argument appears to be a modus ponens; but it is not. Rather, the form of this argument is,

> All *A*s are *B*s.
>
> This is a *C*.
>
> Therefore, this is a *B*.

A moment's reflection should reveal that this form is hardly a valid one.

2.4.4.2 Technically Valid but Still Flawed: *Begging the Question*
Consider the following argument:

> Clarence Thomas emphatically told the Senate that the allegations of his sexual misconduct were lies. Moreover, Clarence Thomas would not lie to the Senate with regard to such an important matter. Therefore, Clarence Thomas told the truth to the Senate.

The careful reader will suspect that something is wrong with this argument even though the argument is technically valid—there is no way for the premises to be true and the conclusion to be false. But this is because the conclusion is also one of the premises! Therefore, making the conclusion false will make at least one of the premises false as well.

This is an instance of arguing in a circle. That which the argument alleges to prove (that is, that Thomas told the truth) is actually assumed to be true, for what is supposedly proven appears in a quasi-concealed form already as a premise. In essence, the argument can be distilled down to this: if we assume that Thomas would not lie to the Senate, we can infer that he told the truth to the Senate. But to tell the truth *is* not to lie! We have already seen that the point of arguing is to convince our audience rationally that an apparently problematic claim is true since it can be inferred from other relatively unproblematic claims. What is the point of arguing when we already assume what we claim to be proving? Arguing in a question-begging manner defeats the purpose of arguing and is as good as not arguing at all. (Indeed, it may be even worse than not arguing at all if it creates the false impression that the speaker is producing good independent reasoning for the conclusion.)

Circular or *question-begging* arguments are (technically) valid arguments, but despite this fact, they are unacceptable and should be rejected upon detection. You should always be on guard for these arguments. The typical question-begging argument is much more subtle and difficult to spot than the blatant example we have provided here.

&ᐣ**A Point of Detail**   There is some controversy among logicians and other philosophers about begging the question—exactly what is it, and exactly what is fallacious about reasoning in this manner? Some say that the conclusion is "already contained" in the premises of any valid deductive argument, and claim that all valid arguments must be question-begging. Our presentation suggests a way to respond: A deductive argument purports to infer the truth of its (problematic) conclusion from a set of unproblematic premises. But if the conclusion already appears as one of the premises, then it appears to be claimed (by the arguer) to be both problematic (since it is the conclusion) and unproblematic (it is a premise). It cannot be both! So a question-begging argument involves either an unproblematic conclusion or a problematic premise, either of which is unacceptable.

TEST YOUR KNOWLEDGE #4

Answer "true" or "false." (If you get less than 90% correct, go back and reread. The answers are at the end of part I.)

_____ 1. All arguments must have at least two premises.

_____ 2. "Clarence Thomas is a Supreme Court justice because he is a Yale graduate" is an argument.

_____ 3. "Clarence Thomas will be a great judge, since he is a Yale graduate" is an argument.

_____ 4. The following is an argument: "In view of the fact that birds fly, the Republicans lost the election. Moreover, birds do fly. Thus, Dole cannot fly."

_____ 5. No inductive arguments are valid.

_____ 6. The following argument is valid: "Since some judges are black and some judges are athletes, it follows that some judges are black athletes."

_____ 7. A sound argument is a strong argument.

_____ 8. Inductive arguments admit of varying degrees of strength.

_____ 9. A sound argument may be invalid.

_____ 10. A sound argument may have a false conclusion.

_____ 11. A valid argument may have false premises and a false conclusion.

_____ 12. The following is a *modus tollens* argument: "If J. J. murdered Nick, he would be found guilty. J. J. was found not-guilty. Thus, J. J. did not murder Nick."

_____ 13. The following is a *modus ponens* argument: "If J. R. did not murder Nick, he would be found not-guilty. J. R. was found not-guilty. Thus, J. R. did not murder Nick."

_____ 14. The following is a *denying the antecedent* argument: "If J. C. did not murder Nick, he would be innocent. J. C. murdered Nick. Thus, J. C. is not innocent."

_____ 15. The following is an *affirming the consequent* argument: "If J. C. did not murder Nick, he would be found not-guilty. J. C. was found not-guilty. Thus, J. C. did not murder Nick."

_____ 16. "She loves me since she told me so, and she would not lie to the people she loves," is a valid argument.

_____ 17. The following is a valid argument: "All laws are principles, and Martha is the principal of her school. So Martha is the law in her school."

_____ 18. "Most lottery tickets are losers, thus probably all lottery tickets are losers" is an invalid argument.

_____ 19. The following is a valid argument: "Either J. C. is a criminal, or he is not a criminal. But he is not a criminal. Thus, he is a criminal."

_____ 20. "Since C. R. is unquestionably one of the most brilliant and exciting justices, the judicial future of this county is well secured" is a weak inductive argument.

2.5 INDUCTIVE REASONING AND METHODS OF APPRAISING STRENGTH

Inductive arguments can be classified in a variety of ways, depending on the pattern they exhibit. We will not attempt here to present a comprehensive picture of all the available inductive patterns, since the significance of each of these varies with different subject matter. For example, one pattern of inductive inference is the so-called "inductive generalization" where we begin with of a *sample* of observed cases that display a certain property and then infer that (probably) *all* similar cases display that property as well. But while inductive generalizations are quite useful in the sciences, they play at most a minor role in the study of law. Thus, we will concentrate in what follows on three kinds of inductive argument that, in order of increasing importance, are indispensable for the study of law. These are:

- Reasoning from authority
- Causal reasoning
- Analogical reasoning

2.5.1 Reasoning from Authority

Reasoning from authority is, perhaps, the easiest form of reasoning encountered in the law. Thus our discussion here is confined to a brief presentation of its structure and the main ways we appraise authority.

2.5.1.1 The Basics
Sometimes a particular claim X is inferred to be true on the grounds that some authority on matters pertaining to X says that X is true. The general pattern of this sort of reasoning is then:

> According to authority A, claim X is true.
> _____
> Therefore, X is true.

Clearly, the conclusion inferred from this type of reasoning is merely probable, since we may be dealing with an illegitimate authority on the matter at hand, or with a legitimate authority who is, nonetheless, biased or simply mistaken about this particular claim. So how do we evaluate arguments from authority?

2.5.1.2 Appraising Arguments from Authority
In general, an argument from authority is no better than the presumed authority on which it relies. So the crucial question here is: what makes an authority (on

a certain matter) a good one? Without distinguishing between persons and "institutional authorities," if we rely on a presumed authority, we must make sure that the following conditions are satisfied:

- **Relevant Expertise**   The presumed authority must be an authority on issues relevant to the subject matter of the argument. For example, we cannot rely on the word of a psychologist when the issue is one of religion, and we cannot rely on the word of a physician for legal matters. Arguments that rely on an appeal to an authority whose expertise does not include the context of the argument commit what logicians call the fallacy of "appeal to [false] authority."
- **Impartiality**   The ideal legitimate authority should be free of bias and prejudices. In practice, of course, ensuring impartiality is a subtle matter. For example, judges frequently "recuse" (disqualify) themselves from a case in which they might appear to have some stake in the case's outcome in order to avoid any suggestion of partiality.
- **Appropriate Credentials**   These may include credentials such as degrees or licenses, hands-on experience, and recognition and respect from other authorities in the area. For example, courts frequently rely on a coroner, who is usually a physician trained in forensic medicine, to establish things such as the time and cause of death.

Failure to satisfy any of these criteria will undermine the legitimacy of the alleged authority at hand. Once again, however, it is not possible to supply a simple formula for determining when an authority has been sufficiently discredited.

💣 **Caution**   In general, you should *not* attempt to discredit an authority by resorting to personal attacks and/or abusive language. These attacks do not discredit the authority and, from a rational point of view, are illegitimate. There are limits to this, however. In the context of assessing the reliability/authority of a witness during a trial, for example, personal attacks prove to be a powerful tool in the hands of a skilled attorney.

2.5.2 Causal Reasoning

We all seem to believe that things do not just happen spontaneously and chaotically, but they happen because they are caused by certain antecedent conditions. But how do we determine what brings about what?

Unfortunately, there is no easy answer to this question. The study of causality and causal reasoning has caused (!) many headaches for scientists and philosophers alike, and a discussion that does justice to the complexity involved in these matters would draw us quickly into the deep and murky waters of philosophy of science, epistemology, and inductive logic. For us that would be a counterproductive diversion. Hence, our treatment of causation will be selective, glancing briefly at only those topics that are most relevant to issues in legal philosophy.

2.5.2.1 The Basics of Causal Reasoning

Causal reasoning is uniform in only one respect: the point of the reasoning (the conclusion of the inference drawn) is always to establish that there is a causal connection between certain events. The nature of a "causal connection" can be either: (a) a claim that there is a causal connection between events of *type E* and events of *type E** (oxidation causes rust), or (b) a claim that a *particular* event *e* is causally connected to a *particular* event *e** (a rusty light switch caused this car's battery to drain). Beyond this, things become more complex, depending on exactly how the conclusion is established or supported.

Fortunately, given our limited concerns here, we can bypass much of the complexity surrounding causality. For unlike science, which is concerned with type-type causal laws and the application of techniques for discovering specific causal connections, what is most important in the law is the judicial determination (and its ramifications) that one particular event is the cause of another particular event. So for our purposes here, the following rudimentary schema of causal reasoning will suffice:

Premise(s): Facts pointing out a correlation between events *e* and *e**.

Conclusion: Events *e* and *e** are causally connected.

Sample Application

In the well-known case of *Palsgraf v. Long Island Railroad,* we find the following application of causal reasoning:

> *Facts:* Two railroad employees are attempting to assist a passenger to board a train that has started to depart; in their attempt to assist the passenger, they pull on his arm and dislodge a package that he was carrying; the package, which contains fireworks, falls on the rails and explodes; the explosion dislodges some nearby scales; the scales fall on and injure Mrs. Palsgraf, a bystander who is waiting at the station to board a train.

> *Conclusion:* The action of the railroad employees caused Mrs. Palsgraf's injuries.

There are several interesting (and very controversial) issues about causality and the law that emerge from *Palsgraf,* and we tackle some of them later in section 3.3.2 and in part III. For now, we must briefly discuss a couple of fundamental issues with regard to the appraisal of causal reasoning.

2.5.2.2 Detecting Weak Causal Reasoning

Causal reasoning itself raises many complex issues, and the issues raised in appraising causal reasoning are equally complex. Although we cannot do justice to the full range of these complexities, we can underscore some frequently encountered pitfalls of causal reasoning. A wide range of weak causal arguments can be easily detected by asking the following questions.

Is the alleged causal connection between events *e* and *e** actually a mere coincidence? Philosophical perplexities aside, causes are temporally prior to their effects. But this can lead some people to reason fallaciously that since event *e* was immediately followed by event *e**, event *e* must be the cause of *e**. (Logicians call this a *post hoc* fallacy.) Of course, mere succession in time between two events hardly suffices to establish a causal connection between them. It would be absurd to conclude, for example, that Simpson's smiling immediately before the jury's verdict was announced caused the jury's decision to acquit him.

Are we ignoring a common cause? Although event *e** may occur immediately after event *e,* and although we may have reason to believe that this is not a coincidence, it can still be that *e* does not cause *e**. It may be that the real cause of both *e** and *e* is a third event *e***. For example, a rise in interest rates followed by a decline in housing sales need not mean that the former is the cause of the latter. Each of these events may have been brought about by a third event, say, a sharp decline in the stock market.

Are we assuming a common cause? There are at least two distinct ways of making this mistake. First, we may erroneously believe that although event *e* is followed by event *e**, *e* is not the cause of *e** but, rather, both *e* and *e** are due to a common third cause *e***. For example, suppose you experience anxiety during the afternoon and insomnia at night. Instead of thinking that the cause of the insomnia is the anxiety, you may think that there is a third, common cause for both the anxiety and the insomnia (say, something you ate for lunch). Second, we may erroneously ignore the possibility of coincidence and assume that there is a common cause for two distinct events *e* and *e**. For example, both a husband and wife may experience insomnia on a given night, but it need not be the case that the very same event (something they ate for dinner) was the common cause for each person's insomnia. It may be, for example, that his insomnia was due to his trying to quit smoking while her insomnia was due to a stressful day at the office.

Is the flow (direction) of causation reversed? Does watching crime shows on TV cause viewers to develop criminal tendencies, or are TV crime shows popular because they cater to the public's latent criminal tendencies? The answer to this is not clear, but the general point of this example should be: when claiming that there is a causal connection between events *e* and *e**, we must be careful to identify the actual flow of causation. We should not confuse the effect with the cause, and vice versa. And it is important to remember that ordinary evidence for causal relations in terms of correlation (for example, the crime rate and the ratings for crime shows rise and fall together) will not establish which causes which, and consequently will not establish which way the "causal arrow" points.

2.5.3 Analogical Reasoning

An Important Warning   Analogical reasoning is central to the law. It cannot be overemphasized that a good understanding of analogical reasoning is crucial for the understanding of legal reasoning in general and of judicial reasoning in particular. We urge you to pay special attention to the material of the next three sections.

2.5.3.1 The Basic Structure

We often compare one thing with a similar thing and reason that given the resemblances between them, some characteristic that we know to be true of one is probably true of the other as well. For example, suppose that you are thinking about enrolling in a philosophy course (logic) taught by professor X. Suppose further that you decide to enroll in that logic course, reasoning that since you liked another philosophy course (metaphysics) you took from X, you will probably enjoy the logic course too. Your reasoning here is something like this:

(1) The course I have taken (metaphysics) and the course that I plan to take (logic) are similar in that they are both philosophy courses and they are both taught by X.

(2) The philosophy course taught by X that I have taken (metaphysics) was an enjoyable one.

Thus, the philosophy course taught by X that I plan to take (logic) will also be an enjoyable one.

That is, on the basis of the known shared properties between both courses (both are in philosophy and both are taught by X) and the known additional property of the metaphysics course that it was an enjoyable one, you conclude that the logic course will resemble it in this respect as well (that is, in being enjoyable).

What we have here is an example of an *analogical inference* (*analogical argument, argument from analogy*). The example is a simple one, involving the comparison of just two things (two courses) that are claimed to resemble each other in only a few respects. Most actual analogies are more complex, comparing one case with (i) a number of cases that it is claimed to resemble in (ii) a number of respects. We should also note that analogical inferences can involve not only philosophy courses, but also objects, events, states of affairs—virtually anything that can be the subject of a comparison.

So let us generalize and introduce some helpful terminology. Analogical arguments typically involve a *comparison group*, a *target case*, and a *target property*. The comparison group consists of a group of cases ($C_1 \ldots C_n$), all of which we know to share a common set of properties ($F_1 \ldots F_n$). The target case is also known to possess the properties $F_1 \ldots F_n$), thus it resembles the cases in the comparison group. We are unsure whether the target case possesses some additional property (F_{n+1}), the target property, but we know that each member of the comparison group does possess the target property. We can then outline the general schema of analogical inference as follows:

GENERAL SCHEMA OF ANALOGICAL INFERENCE

(1) All cases $C_1 \ldots C_n$ in a comparison group and a target case, C_{n+1}, have in common properties $F_1 \ldots F_n$.

(2) All cases $C_1 \ldots C_n$ in the comparison group also have the additional target property F_{n+1}.

∴(3) Probably, the target case C_{n+1} also has F_{n+1}.

Sample Application

Consider the following simple hypothetical scenario. Suppose you are an attorney who is consulting with a client who wishes to sue her employer for injuries inflicted by defective machinery used in performing her customary duties. Your client tells you that she knows of several cases in which workers sustained job-related injuries under circumstances very similar to her own, and that in each of these cases the injured worker received compensation from his/her employer. On the basis of these facts alone, your client infers that she too will receive compensation from her employer. Using our terminology, the client's reasoning yields the following concrete instance of the general schema of analogical inference:

(1) All the cases I know of (that is, the comparison group) and my case (that is, the target case) have in common the properties of involving an employee who is injured by defective machinery while performing his/her customary duties.

(2) All the cases I know of also have the additional (target) property of the injured employee receiving compensation for his/her injuries from his/her employer.

(3) *Therefore,* probably, in my case I will also be compensated for my injuries.

2.5.3.2 Appraising Analogical Inferences

Analogical inferences are *inductive* ones. The premises provide some support for the conclusion, but the conclusion follows only with some degree of *probability,* and never with certainty (as in valid deductive inferences). How then do we determine the probability of the conclusion (and thus the relative strength) of a particular analogical argument?

Although there is no mechanical formula for precisely measuring the strength of a particular analogical argument, logicians have identified several factors that can determine the relative strength of analogical arguments. We begin by considering two of these factors that focus on the comparison group alone:

1. **The size of the comparison group:** the greater the number of the cases in the comparison group, the stronger the argument.

and

2. **The homogeneity/heterogeneity of the comparison group:**
   the more diversified (heterogeneous) the comparison group, the
   stronger the argument; the more uniform (homogeneous) the comparison group, the weaker the argument.

Comment   In general, it should be obvious that to secure a fair comparison group (in the statistical, nonmoral sense of the term *fair*), we are better off
comparing the target case with more rather than fewer cases. Thus, in the
Sample Application case presented earlier, if your client tells you that she knows
of *several* similar cases, on the basis of factor 1 alone you can say to your client
that her case appears stronger than it would if she had knowledge of fewer
cases. Similarly, the argument is stronger if it includes a more varied and diverse
comparison group. This gives us increased confidence that the target property is
not merely an accidental one and, therefore, that the target case will have it. In
the example of the injured worker, let us assume that (i) you have found a large
number of court decisions on worker injury where the court decided for the
plaintiff, and that (ii) these cases are quite diverse—some involve the private sec-
tor and some the public one, the working conditions varied in each case, the
injury involved was caused not only by machinery but also by all sorts of instru-
ments, and so on. According to factor 2, the increased heterogeneity of the comparison group provides additional support for the claim that your client will
recover. Thus, on the basis of factors 1 and 2 so far, your client appears to have
a strong case. But this is not the end of the story.

💣 **Caution**   Both factors 1 and 2 focus on *the comparison group only.*
But we should not be too quick to judge an analogical inference strong
just because it is based on a large and/or "fair" comparison group. Just
one "killer" dissimilarity between the comparison group and the target
case can render an analogy worthless regardless of the large size or the
otherwise representative character of the comparison group. For example, your client may have conveniently forgotten to mention that in all the
cases in which the plaintiff recovered, the workers were found not to be
negligent while performing their duties, whereas in her case, she was
intoxicated at the time she was injured. Factors 1 and 2 may not mean
much if there are important dissimilarities between the comparison
group and the target case. Consequently, perhaps the most important factor in appraising analogical arguments focuses on the similarities/dissim-
ilarities *between the comparison group and the target case.* Thus, the
main criterion of evaluation of analogical arguments is the following:

3. **The relevant similarities/dissimilarities between the comparison group and the target case:** the greater the similarity,
   the stronger the argument is; and the greater the dissimilarity, the
   weaker the argument is.

Comment   The similarity of the target case to the cases in the comparison
group is a factor that *strengthens* an analogical inference. In the example we

have been using, suppose that you have found a number of cases judged in favor of the plaintiff where the facts were very similar to those in your client's case. For example, in each comparison case, the injured person shared with your client the same line of work, equipment used, and working conditions. The close similarity between your client's case and the cases in the comparison group strengthens the inference that in your client's case, the court will also find for the plaintiff. By contrast, if we suppose that there are significant dissimilarities between the cases in which the court decided in favor of the plaintiff and your client's case (for example, your client was intoxicated, while those who recovered were not), then this factor weakens your inference that in your client's case, the court will also find for the plaintiff.

💣 **Caution**   There are three closely related points that cannot be overemphasized:

- *There is no mechanical formula for identifying similarities and dissimilarities.* With a bit of ingenuity, similarities and differences can be found at will. Consider again the injured-worker example. We could ask the following questions about the target case and the comparison group: at what time of day did the injuries occur, what was the weather like at the time of the injuries, what day of the week was it, what time of day was it, and what type of clothing were the injured workers wearing? In short, each property that is true of the target case or the members of the comparison group (and there may be an indefinite number of such properties) can establish a similarity or difference. This brings us to a second, related point.
- *The strength (and weakness) of an analogical inference is not simply a function of the number of similarities (and differences) between the target case and the comparison group.* Although it is true that in general, similarities "make" an analogy and dissimilarities "break" an analogy, assessing an analogy's strength is not a strictly quantitative matter. Returning again to the injured-worker example, a multitude of similarities between your client's case and other cases in which plaintiffs recovered (all workers were between the ages of 40 and 50, were wearing a company uniform, had more than five years' experience, and so on) can be outweighed *by just one "killer" dissimilarity;* perhaps your client was drunk, and every worker who recovered was sober. Indeed, that difference *by itself* might be sufficient to defeat the analogy. This brings us to a third important point.
- *Similarities/dissimilarities must be relevant.* Simply identifying similarities (to strengthen the analogy) or dissimilarities (to weaken the analogy) between the target case and the comparison group does not get us anywhere if what we point to is not relevant in the context. But what makes a similarity (or dissimilarity) relevant to a given analogy? Relevance is normally cashed out in *causal* terms:

the similarities (or dissimilarities) between the comparison cases and the target case should be *causally relevant* to the target property. For example, in the injured-worker case, suppose you are attempting to assess whether your client's impaired vision contributed to her accident, and that you do so on the basis of an apparently closely analogous case. It should be obvious that some similarities between both cases—such as both injured persons being married, both having children, both driving the same kind of car, and both being Catholics—are irrelevant to the target property in question (impaired vision as a cause of the accident) and do *not* strengthen the analogy. Likewise, irrelevant dissimilarities (wearing a black versus a blue shirt; one likes cheese pizza, the other mushroom) do *not* weaken the analogy. Of course, what is and what is not causally relevant in a specific case may not always be obvious (recall the difficulties we mentioned regarding causal inferences). Although sometimes the causal relations involved are matters of common knowledge, quite often we have to rely on expert opinion.

Moreover, even when the similarities (or differences) are apparently determined to be causally relevant to the target property, their exact role and significance in a given case may not be entirely obvious. For example, suppose that in the case of the two workers, both of those injured had impaired vision. Yet, one injured person wore contacts, while the other injured person wore bifocals. One was nearsighted, while the other was farsighted. One had an eye operation a month before the accident, but the other did not. One was taking medication that can cause blurred vision, while the other was not. A seemingly endless number of these examples can always be produced. For this reason, the exact causal impact of each relevant similarity or difference has to be assessed individually and always in

---

A Simple Analogy?

In August 1999, Senator Phil Gramm, R-Texas, chairman of the Senate Banking Committee, demonstrated his confidence in the banking system's ability to handle the Y2K problem as follows:

> Well, it seems to me we ought to be encouraged that in the year 1000, they had to add a new digit, and yet no evidence of economic disruption. And then a millennium before, we had dates going down, and then they started going up, and yet no evidence of disruption or chaos in the economy. So, if they could do it then, surely we can deal with it now, it seems to me.

> *The Washington Post*

How would you evaluate the reasoning here?

context. And we cannot overemphasize the point that determining genuine causal relations is no simple matter.

2.5.3.3 Refuting an Analogy

We begin this section with one important piece of advice: never try to refute an analogy until you understand each specific feature of that analogy. That is, one must know the nature of the comparison group, the details of the target case, and the specifics of the target property. To this effect, it can be helpful to rewrite the argument as a concrete instance of the general pattern of analogical arguments.

In legal contexts, the following two general methods of refuting an analogical argument are most common.

The Straightforward Way—Appealing to Weakening Factors The direct way of refuting an analogy is to appeal to the methods of appraisal discussed in the previous section and show that the analogy is a weak one. Particularly crucial to this method is factor 3: we point to *relevant dissimilarities* between the target case and the comparison group. If we succeed in establishing that there are relevant dissimilarities, we succeed in weakening the argument. Always remember that simply identifying dissimilarities is not enough. The dissimilarities must be relevant and important enough to inflict serious damage on the proposed analogy—they must be strong enough to weaken the analogical inference. Once again, in the injured-worker example, if the worker was drunk, and all workers who recovered were sober, this would be both a relevant and significant dissimilarity that would seriously weaken the analogical inference.

The Indirect Way—Constructing a Counteranalogy An indirect way of refuting a given analogy is to "ignore" your opponent's analogical inference and present instead your own competing analogy whose conclusion is *contradictory* (see section 1.3.3) to that of your opponent's analogy. If you succeed in establishing your own analogy, it follows that your opponent's position *must* be false. This strategy is very common in legal contexts. Often the plaintiff and defendant try to find prior cases that they argue to be relevantly similar to theirs, and that support their side of the argument. Indeed, the whole outcome of the case can turn on which analogy is judged stronger. Consider again the injured-worker case, and suppose that you are the attorney for the defense and you are confronted with the following analogy advanced in court by the plaintiff's attorney:

> In cases *A, B, C,* the court found for the plaintiff. The case before us is relevantly similar to *A, B, C.* Thus, you should find for the plaintiff.

As the attorney for the defense, you may choose to employ the method of counteranalogy and argue against your opponent as follows:

> In cases *D, E, F,* the court found for the defendant. The case before us is relevantly similar to *D, E, F.* Thus, you should find for the defendant.

The court must then determine whether the case before it is more like the comparison cases *A, B, C,* or more like the comparison cases *D, E, F* (that is, decide the relative strength of the analogies between the present case and either *A, B,*

C or *D, E, F*). If the verdict is returned for the defendant, you would have refuted the plaintiff's attorney's analogy.

TO THINK ABOUT

Consider the following two conflicting judicial rulings (modified from actual cases):

No Liability for Trespassers Rule: Ordinarily, the owner of premises owes no duty to keep his premises safe for trespassers, though the latter be infants.

Rule of the Turntable Cases (Attractive Nuisance Rule): The owner of dangerous machinery so situated and exposed on his premises that it will naturally attract children, who cannot understand the dangers involved from its use, who takes no precautions to prevent access to it is liable for negligence should a child be injured by the use of such machinery.

Assume that the former was the ruling in some case *X* and that the latter was the ruling in a different case *Y*, and suppose the following (true) scenario. An eleven-year-old boy trespasses on the land of his neighbor and drowns in a pond of water that is usually formed during the rainy season on that land. The attorney of the father of the boy sues the owner of the pond for damages and claims that there should be a finding for the plaintiff, since this case is like case *Y*. When the case reaches the appeals court, the judge provides the following reasoning:

A turntable [that is, a rotating platform equipped with a railway truck that is used for turning locomotives] is not only a danger specially created by the act of the owner but it is a danger of a different kind to those which exist in the order of nature. A pond, although artificially created, is in nowise different from those natural ponds and streams, which exist everywhere, and which involve the same dangers and present the same appearance and the same attractions to children. A turntable can be rendered absolutely safe, without destroying or materially impairing its usefulness, by simply locking it. A pond cannot be rendered inaccessible to boys by any ordinary means. Certainly no ordinary fence around the lot upon which a pond is situated would answer the purpose; and therefore, to make it safe, it must either be filled or drained, or, in other words, destroyed. But ponds are always useful, and often necessary, and where they do not exist naturally must be created, in order to store water for stock and for domestic purposes, irrigation, etc. Are we to hold that every owner of a pond or reservoir is liable in damages for any child that comes uninvited upon his premises and happens to fall in the water and drown? If so, then upon the same principle must the owner of a fruit tree be held liable for the death or injury of a child who, attracted by the fruit, climbs into the branches, and falls out. But this, we imagine, is an absurdity, for which no one would contend, and it proves that the rule of the Turntable Cases does not rest upon a principle so broad and of such rigid application as counsel supposes. The owner of a thing dangerous and attractive to children is not always and universally liable for an injury to a child tempted by the attraction.

From Justice Beatty's opinion in *Peters v. Bowman,*
115 Cal. 345, 47 P. 598 (1897)

First, assess and evaluate the reasoning of the court in this case. Then decide who (and why) should be the victor in this case.

TEST YOUR KNOWLEDGE #5

Answer "true" or "false." (If you get less than 90% correct, go back and reread. The answers are at the end of part I.)

_____ 1. The basic criterion of evaluating an argument from authority is the number of authorities that figure in the premises.

_____ 2. Suppose George says: "Clarence Thomas's opinions on affirmative action must not be taken seriously, since Thomas became a Supreme Court judge exactly because he is black." George has successfully cast doubt on the legitimacy of Thomas's authority on issues of affirmative action.

_____ 3. The following is a strong argument: "According to Jay Leno, the level of education of black people in the inner cities is very poor. Thus, probably, the level of education of black people in the inner cities is very poor."

_____ 4. The following is a weak argument: "Former president Reagan said that homeless people live in the streets by choice. Thus, homeless people choose to be homeless."

_____ 5. The following is a strong argument: "Sigmund Freud, the father of psychoanalysis, said that organized religion is a socially bad idea. Thus, organized religion is a socially bad idea."

_____ 6. The following argument is an instance of causal reasoning: "Poverty causes crime, and crime causes poverty. Thus, poverty causes poverty."

_____ 7. The following is a strong causal argument: "Twenty different people I know lost money every time they gambled in a casino on a Good Friday. So, probably, we should avoid playing in casinos on Good Fridays."

_____ 8. The following argument is a weak one: "Statistics show that most violent criminals watch many hours of violent TV shows. Thus, violent TV shows cause violent crimes."

_____ 9. The most important factor in evaluating an analogical argument is the number of similarities/dissimilarities that exist among the members of the comparison group.

_____ 10. The greater the number of similarities between the comparison group and the target case, the stronger the analogical argument.

ANSWERS TO TEST YOUR KNOWLEDGE QUESTIONS IN PART I

Test #1

1. F	6. T
2. F	7. F
3. F	8. F
4. F	9. F
5. F	10. T

Test #2

1. F	6. T
2. T	7. T
3. T	8. T
4. T	9. F
5. T	10. F

Test #3

1. T	5. F	9. F	13. T	17. F
2. T	6. F	10. F	14. T	18. T
3. F	7. F	11. F	15. F	19. T
4. F	8. F	12. F	16. F	20. F

Test #4

1. F	5. T	9. F	13. F	17. F
2. F	6. F	10. F	16. T	18. T
3. T	7. F	11. T	15. T	19. F
4. F	8. T	12. T	14. T	20. F

Test #5

1. F	6. F
2. F	7. F
3. F	8. T
4. T	9. F
5. F	10. T

PART II

ELEMENTS OF LEGAL REASONING

CHAPTER 3

REASONING AND THE LAW

3.1 THE CENTRALITY OF REASONING IN THE LAW

The idea that logic and reasoning are prominently involved in the law seems so obvious that it needs no argument at all. Reasoning, the process of justifying a claim on the basis of reasons provided for that claim, has a central and indisputable position in legal contexts as varied as a person's everyday ordinary experiences with the law, the process of making law, and applying existing law to specific situations. Consider the following relatively simple illustrations:

Reasoning Involved in Personal Experiences with the Law   Whether we like it or not, each of us is constantly exposed to reasoning in legal contexts. On a daily basis, we read and hear about argumentative debates in the legislature, and we are bombarded with news reports about attorneys arguing their case in the press and judges and juries reasoning their way through complex, high-profile trials. And, certainly, we think about how the law directly affects our actions in some way every day. Many people, for example, abstain from committing a crime due to such reasoning as the following:

> If I commit a crime, I will end up in jail.
>
> I will commit a crime.
> _____
> Therefore, I will end up in jail.

A simple modus ponens, along with the normal human reluctance to end up in jail, provides a good reason (although perhaps not the *best* reason) for maintaining law and order!

Reasoning Involved in Making Laws   We constantly make new laws. But when we consider the merits of adopting of a new law, argumentation plays a most crucial role. Suppose, for example, that there is currently no law requiring children to wear bicycle helmets. Assume moreover that the American Medical Association (AMA), acting on the belief that we ought to prevent unnecessary injuries and/or deaths of children, convinces the legislature to hold hearings to consider the merits of adopting such a law. What would be the major content of such hearings? Obviously, *arguments* regarding the pros and cons of bicycle helmet legislation. The AMA might testify, for example, that we can save children from serious injury and even death by implementing such a law; some parents may share the concerns of the AMA, while other parents might argue that this constitutes an illegitimate intrusion by the government into what are private family matters; legal authorities might point out the difficulty they would face in enforcing such a law (would they have to cite, arrest, and incarcerate helmetless, bike-riding children?); and some might argue that the policy would place an unfair burden on the poor who cannot afford high-priced helmets.

Reasoning Involved in Applying the Law   In the 1990s, the so-called "veggie libel" laws were enacted in more than a dozen states after growers suffered losses in the wake of a 1989 report about apples and the pesticide Alar. The purported intention of the enacting legislatures was to provide recourse for farmers and ranchers when their products were attacked with unsubstantiated claims. Nonetheless, it was never made clear what exactly one was prohibited from doing or saying according to these statutes. Could, for example, one speak ill of a kind of food on a television talk show? The laws were tested in the spring of 1998 when a group of Texas cattlemen brought a lawsuit against the popular TV host Oprah Winfrey for allegedly violating the Texas food disparagement law. They claimed that Oprah's televised comments that "mad cow" disease "stopped her cold from eating another hamburger" caused the beef market to plummet and cost them millions of dollars. The case was litigated and received much attention, since it was the first court test of veggie libel laws whose outcome would influence food producers, food-safety groups, the media, and consumers.

The actual details of the litigation do not concern us here. What we must observe, nonetheless, is that every aspect of the litigation depends upon someone engaging in reasoning. For instance, the attorneys for the cattlemen had what they took to be good reasons for filing the suit; they must have thought that some purpose of theirs would be served by doing it (for example, they might have wanted to deter others from making such comments about their cattle). At the trial itself, argumentation would be everywhere. We would expect the cattlemen's attorneys to argue that no one should be permitted to speak ill of a food product without being able to provide proof, and that Oprah's remarks were unsubstantiated. They would maintain that her remarks clearly broke a law intended to protect farmers and ranchers from reckless statements suggesting that a food product is not safe for consumption. Similarly, Oprah's attorneys would probably argue that veggie libel laws were put in place by the agribusiness industry to intimidate and, contrary to the First Amendment, to silence critical discussion of food-safety issues. They might add that their client's comments did not constitute a violation of these laws anyway, since they were neither reckless nor without foundation. Most importantly, as we will see in some detail in section 3.4, the judge hearing the case would engage in lengthy and complex reasoning in order to decide the case. Indeed, the hallmark of adjudication within a legal system like ours is that determinations such as whether a person violated a legal prohibition depend on arguments that contain reasons for concluding that the prohibition has or has not been violated.

Our purpose here is not to provide an exhaustive list of legal contexts in which reasons and argument play a role, but rather to illustrate how important reasoning is in the law. To be sure, there have been skeptics about the importance of reasoning, and even of logic in general, in the law. The great jurist Oliver Wendell Holmes's infamous remark that "the life of the law has not been logic; it has been experience" has been quoted in numerous texts, articles, and judicial opinions. But it seems to us that the contemporary jurist George Fletcher gets the better of the argument with Justice Holmes with the following response: "The life of the law may not be logic, but unresolved contradictions would initiate its demise." Which is to say, logic may not be definitive of the law (that is, may not be both a necessary and sufficient condition for the law), but it is undoubtedly a necessary condition without which law and legal procedures could not exist.

3.2 DEDUCTIVE REASONING AND THE LAW

Given that reasoning is indispensable to the law, and that deduction is central to reasoning in general, we should expect to encounter deductive reasoning in virtually every area of the law. We shall confine ourselves to a single, albeit highly controversial, issue, the role of deduction in *legal reasoning,* when legal reasoning is narrowly construed as *judicial reasoning,* the reasoning of judges when they decide actual cases.

To understand the role of deduction in legal reasoning, consider first an extralegal example. In a typical college course, the final grade is normally determined on the basis of the course's "rules of grading," that is, announcements by the instructor—usually in the syllabus—of what criteria need to be satisfied to get an A, a B, and so on. Suppose that in one course, a *sufficient condition* (section 1.3.2.3.2) for passing is attaining a grade of C or better on each of the exams. Suppose that George has received a grade of B on every exam. From a simple application of deductive reasoning, it now follows with *deductive certainty* (section 2.3.1) that George has passed the class.

Though more rigorous than ordinary deductive reasoning, legal reasoning in its deductive form seems to follow the same pattern as in our simple example. That is, a judge's deductive legal reasoning characteristically involves (a) recognizing an authoritative rule of law, (b) identifying the legally relevant facts of the case in a way that "fits the rule," and then (c) applying the rule to the facts so as to reach the proper legal conclusion. In the law, the deductive pattern of the application of a legal rule to the facts of a case is called, in a rather archaic fashion, a *syllogism,* and is supposed to involve the following:

A major premise: A statute or rule of law applying to the case at hand.

A minor premise: The legally relevant facts in the specific case at hand (that is, the facts of the case that purportedly "fit" the rule cited in the major premise).

The conclusion: The judgment of the court. (In a civil case, the conclusion might be about whether a legal remedy is or is not appropriate; in a criminal case, the conclusion might be about punishment.)

Here is a simple illustration:

> *Major premise:* Wills witnessed by fewer than two people are invalid.
>
> *Minor premise:* George's will was signed by just one witness.
>
> ---
>
> *Conclusion:* George's will is invalid.

You may be tempted to think at this point that the "legal syllogism" is a distinct pattern of reasoning completely unrelated to anything we examined in our brief treatment of elementary logic in part I. But a moment's reflection reveals that the "syllogism" is not really some monstrous beast concocted by lawyers to confuse the rest of us. First, our discussion of *conditional statements* pointed out that *general statements* of the form "All *A*s are *B*s" can be viewed as conditionals that assert roughly, "If you have an instance of an *A*, then you have an instance of a *B*" (section 1.3.2.3.3). Second, legal rules are typically general statements, and thus translate as conditionals. In our example, the rule "Wills witnessed by fewer than two people are invalid" translates as "If a will is witnessed by fewer than two witnesses, then that will is invalid." Third, recall our characterization of the pattern of reasoning we called *modus ponens* (section 2.4.2.1): it involves as premises a conditional statement and the antecedent of that statement, and as a conclusion the consequent of that conditional. Now, returning to our example, the rule of law is our conditional, and the "minor premise" is the antecedent of that conditional, namely, "George's will was witnessed by fewer than two people." The conclusion "George's will is invalid" follows with deductive validity. In the end, the "legal syllogism" turns out to be a "camouflaged" modus ponens, a pattern of reasoning that we should all find familiar and unthreatening.

How important are deductive "syllogisms" in legal reasoning? The quick answer is that deductive reasoning is a perfect fit for the application of the law, for is not the law a "bunch of rules," such as statutes, codes, and regulations enacted by appropriate legislative authorities? And is not the proper task of the courts to apply the rule to a particular set of facts?

Well, yes and no. To be sure, the view that legal reasoning is dominated by the deductive process of applying specific rules to specific sets of facts has many advantages: given that the value of valid deductions is the establishment of solid, unshakable conclusions (section 2.3.1), we now increase the level of certainty in the law. Moreover, this view accords well with the *principle of legislative supremacy,* a principle that results from our acceptance of the doctrine of separation of powers (Appendix II.2.1) and that dictates that the proper role of the judiciary is applying laws that originate in the legislative branch as opposed to "legislating from the bench." On the other hand, there are several difficulties facing this view. In brief:

- *The law involves more than just rules.* As some critics of *legal formalism* (section 3.4.3.1) have gone to great lengths to demonstrate, the law is more than a "bunch of rules," and the judicial decision goes beyond the simple application of "mechanistic" rules to unambiguous facts.

Political, moral, prudential, and other considerations also play a role in the law, and the role of the personal preferences of judges cannot be ignored.

- *There are problems with the rules.* There may be no appropriate rule that covers a case (especially an unanticipated, novel case), and there may be conflicts among equally applicable rules. Moreover, existing rules may contain *ambiguous* and/or *vague* language (section 1.2.1) that requires interpretation. Indeed, as Professor Edward Levi has observed, "In an important sense legal rules are never clear, and, if a rule had to be clear before it could be imposed, society would be impossible." We explore this important issue in section 3.4.1.1.

- *There are problems with the facts.* The application of deductive reasoning requires a statement of the facts in the "minor premise." But the description of the facts of a case is never a straightforward issue. For one thing, the facts can be described narrowly or broadly, and each description might be equally correct. We will see more of this important problem in section 3.4.

- *Deduction is a "late comer."* The application of the "syllogistic" deductive model of judicial reasoning presupposes that the court has (i) identified the legally relevant facts of the case, (ii) determined exactly which legal rule applies to that case, and (iii) determined how that legal rule applies to those facts. Obviously the distinctive features of judicial reasoning involve determining the relevant facts, determining the appropriate rule, and fitting the rule to the facts (almost anyone could do the simple modus ponens if all of this was in place). But none of these distinctive aspects of legal reasoning involves the deductive model itself. The deductive model comes into play only after these important determinations are already in place, and the deductive model provides no guidance for making these determinations. Thus, for the most part, the most controversial and distinctive features of legal reasoning are independent of the deductive model of applying legal rules to specific facts.

All in all, it should be clear that an accurate and thorough picture of legal reasoning requires looking beyond deduction to induction as well.

3.3 INDUCTIVE REASONING AND THE LAW

The most obvious role for induction within legal contexts lies in determining the facts of a case during a trial. Legal proceedings are usually initiated by an allegation or complaint that some set of events or circumstances has occurred, for which the legal system should impose a punishment or provide a remedy in light of these facts. Sometimes the essence of a legal dispute concerns only the facts themselves—the state claims Jones robbed a convenience store, and Jones claims he did not. The court listens to eyewitness accounts and expert testimony, admits documents into evidence, and attempts to determine, to the best of its ability and according to fairly strict *rules of evidence,* what (if anything) happened that raises an issue for the legal system.

But the role of inductive reasoning in the law is hardly limited to fact finding. The various forms of inductive reasoning we encountered in chapter 2 play a prominent—indeed often dominant—role in every aspect of legal procedures in general and in legal reasoning in particular.

3.3.1 Authority and the Law

The use of authorities (or at least presumed authorities) and *reasoning from authority* (section 2.5.1.1) occur both in settling questions of fact during a trial and in determining what the law is in a specific case.

The Use of Authority in Determining the Facts of a Case   A principal objective for a trial court is settling *questions of fact.* But a determination of the facts requires reasoned examination of the *evidence,* which in turn relies extensively on the authoritative *testimony of witnesses.* Trials usually include the examination and cross-examination of "firsthand authorities," including eyewitnesses, arresting officers, and others who have firsthand acquaintance with the events in question. Similarly, *expert witnesses,* persons who have no firsthand knowledge of the case at hand, but are recognized by the court as a legitimate authority on some matter relevant to the case at hand, are often called to provide the court with their judgment. Of course, the legitimacy of the presumed authority in a given case is subject to the *methods of appraisal of authorities* (section 2.5.1.2), and the admission of all testimony is regulated by the elaborate system of rules of evidence. But as long as expert (or other) testimony satisfies the conditions of legitimacy of authority and accords with the rules of evidence, it provides the trial court with inductive grounds for the truth of a claim under dispute and is an integral constituent of the trial.

The Use of Authority in Determining What the Law Is   In addressing *questions of law,* that is, what the law is on a specific matter, courts (and others) rely on authorities—recognized *authoritative sources of law.* In general, in the American legal system, two indisputable sources of legal authority are *statutes* (pieces of legislation passed by recognized legislative bodies) and prior *judicial decisions.* The reason statutory law is an authoritative source of law is straightforward: the judiciary has a duty, under the doctrine of separation of powers (Appendix II.2.1), to make decisions by applying the (constitutional) bills passed by the legislature. The reason past judicial decisions are a legally authoritative source, on the other hand, is a more complex matter that requires separate treatment. We examine this issue in section 3.3.3.

There are many ways of classifying the authorities that a court can rely on or invoke in support of its decision. For instance, authorities can be *primary* (within the law—a constitutional provision, statute, judicial opinions, administrative regulations) or *secondary* (outside the law—law review articles, legal encyclopedias, other legal texts). A *mandatory* authority is something on which a court must rely in reaching its decision. Only primary authorities are mandatory authorities. They include enacted law and other court opinions. Courts are required to follow other judicial opinions when those opinions are sufficiently similar to the case before the court, and if the opinions were written by a higher court. A *persuasive* authority is something that the court is not required to rely on, but which it may choose to rely on in reaching its decision. This can include secondary authorities and prior court opinions that the court is not required to follow (perhaps from another jurisdiction or even another country), but which it finds persuasive.

Even though some materials are claimed to have binding force within the law or to be legally binding (bills and their amendments, the Constitution and its amendments, judicial holdings), their content, scope, and weight may be controversial, and there is no single rule for determining any of these. There are general formulas—for example, the Constitution is the highest law (if something else conflicts with it, the Constitution wins); statute overrides precedent (Congress passed the Food and Drug Act because the courts did not hold companies liable according to the common law precedents of torts, and from that point on companies were held liable); federal law preempts state law (any state that passed a law exempting its residents from federal income tax would find this out quickly enough); and the Supreme Court has the final say in applying the Constitution (it has held that the right to free speech is not absolute, and on this basis has upheld statutes that prohibit publishing sensitive state secrets). But formulations such as these are very general and do not settle the sort of very specific questions that legal cases often raise (for example, do civil rights laws prohibit discrimination against homosexuals in public housing? in the armed services?). So even though there are fairly detailed rules that spell out what counts as an authority and how courts are to employ authorities in their reasoning, legal reasoning that involves authorities often gives rise to controversy and disagreement.

3.3.2 Causality and the Law

In our discussion of *causal reasoning* (section 2.5.2.2), we observed that causality itself is a highly complex issue. The treatment of causality within the law adds further layers of complexity, so our discussion here must be highly selective. We will glance briefly at only two issues: how specific causes are assessed in the law, and the connection between causality and legal responsibility.

The Meaning of "Cause" in Legal Contexts—Assessing Specific Causes   The goal of most causal reasoning in the law is the establishment of a causal connection between two specific events. The significant question for a court is whether this particular event e is the cause of that particular event e^*. But exactly what is the *legal meaning* of the expression "event e is the *cause* of event e^*"? The answer is that in the law, there are at least two "standard" ways of understanding this expression, depending on the context.

In simpler cases involving just one causal entity (for example, Art, acting alone, shoots Bob who dies instantly), a court seeking to answer a *cause-in-fact* question (who caused what?) will normally assess the issue by employing the concept of cause as a *necessary condition* (section 1.3.2.3.2), and applying the following test:

The *but-for test* (or *sine qua non* rule)

For the defendant's act to be the cause-in-fact of the plaintiff's injury, it must be shown that the injury would not have occurred without that act. That is, the act must be a necessary condition of the injury. Contrapositively: if the plaintiff's injury would have occurred anyway without the defendant's harmful act, then the defendant's act is not the cause-in-fact of the injury.

Suppose, for example, that Art is recklessly driving while intoxicated; he loses control of his car and hits Bob, a pedestrian on a sidewalk. Bob suffers a massive heart attack and dies instantly. To determine cause-in-fact by applying the but-for test is to ask the following question: Would Bob have died but for (had it not been for) Art's car hitting him? If the answer to this question is no, then we know that had it not been for the reckless way Art drove, Bob would not have suffered a fatal heart attack, and Art is thus the cause-in-fact of Bob's death. But suppose we find that Bob would have died regardless of Art's careless driving (he was suffering from heart problems that would have caused a massive heart attack anyway at the time he was hit by Art's car). Then the but-for test yields that Art is not the cause of Bob's death.

Understanding legal cause as a necessary condition and applying the but-for test, though common in the law, are not always adequate for determining cause-in-fact. To see this, let us consider a more troublesome case. Suppose that Art and Bob both shoot at Charlie, and each of their bullets hits Charlie, who dies instantly. At the trial Art claims that according to the but-for test, he is not the cause of Charlie's death: regardless of Art's bullet hitting him, Charlie would have died anyway (from Bob's bullet hitting him). So Art's shooting him is not the cause-in-fact of Charlie's death. But the problem is that Bob invokes the same defense: would Charlie have died had it not been for Bob's bullet hitting him? Of course he would have, Bob asserts. Art's bullet would have killed him anyway, regardless of Bob's own shooting. So by the but-for test, Bob's shooting him is not the cause-in-fact of Charlie's death either. But now the application of the but-for test by Art and Bob shows that neither Art's nor Bob's actions caused Charlie's death! Surely something has gone wrong.

As this example demonstrates, we cannot always view causes simply as necessary conditions. Thus courts have adopted criteria for assessing causes that focus on whether something is a *material factor* or a *substantial factor* in bringing about something else. The specific criteria for these determinations are both complex and controversial, consuming large portions of law-school courses, and are clearly beyond our present scope. But this much is clear: something need not be a necessary condition to be either a material or substantial factor in bringing something about, nor need it be the *only* factor. (It need not be a *sufficient condition,* either section 1.3.2.3.2, but that is yet another complexity that we gloss over.) Employing the analysis of cause in terms of material and substantial factors, courts would be able to conclude, in our previous example, that both Art's and Bob's shooting Charlie were material and substantial factors in bringing about Charlie's death, and therefore hold both Art and Bob legally liable.

Why Causes Matter in the Law—Proximate Causes and Legal Responsibility   Causality matters in the law because issues of causality are intricately related to issues of legal responsibility in both private and public law. Although *A*'s violating a legal rule within the criminal code or causing harm to *B* would not be sufficient for holding *A* legally responsible (perhaps his mental condition excuses him), it remains that *A*'s causing harm to *B* is a necessary condition in (nearly) all cases of tort liability, and *A*'s violating some legal rule is a necessary condition for most cases of criminal liability

Let us turn our attention to *tort liability.* Torts involve claims that one's negligent (or otherwise legally faulty) conduct has resulted in injuries (to another's body, property, reputation) for which the injured party is owed a legal remedy (Appendix II.1.3 and II.1.4). But this nearly always requires the court to determine that the injuries in question *were actually caused* by the faulty behavior of the defendant. More specifically, in order to establish the defendant's negligence toward the plaintiff, it must be shown that (a) the defendant had a *legal duty* to exercise reasonable care and therefore to refrain from the (usually excessively risky) behavior in question, (b) the defendant *failed to comply* with that duty, and (c) the defendant's failure to comply with the duty is the *cause* of the plaintiff's injury.

Establishing that the defendant caused the plaintiff's injuries is a crucial and arguably indispensable component of the assessment of liability. But here a crucial clarification is necessary. Causes come in chains: events are caused by prior events, which in turn have been caused by even prior events, and so on. Consider our earlier example in which Art's car injured Bob. It can be argued that the accident would not have happened but for Art's driving carelessly, which in turn would not have happened but for Art's heavy drinking in a bar earlier, which would not have happened but for Art's wife abandoning him, which would not have happened but for the argument they had a week earlier, and so on. Which event is the cause of Bob's injury? If the injury would not have occurred but for the careless driving or the drinking or the abandonment or the argument, the "but-for" test will be unable to identify any of these as the unique cause of Bob's injury. In theory, this process can go backward in time indefinitely; so if a court is ever to decide a case involving liability, it needs to locate a "cutoff" point in the causal chain and declare it *the* (legal) cause in that case.

The way the courts customarily deal with this problem is by drawing a distinction between *proximate* (nearby) causes and *distant* (remote) causes, and limiting their consideration to only proximate causes. And the way courts "discover" proximate causes is, in theory, even simpler: they locate a specific point in the causal chain (a) that is not too remote in time, (b) at which it can be shown that the defendant could have *foreseen* the risk of injury to the plaintiff, and (c) at which the injury was probable.

Notice that foreseeability of harm from the risk created by the defendant's action(s) is a crucial element in the determination of proximate causes, and thus it is a crucial element in the analysis of legal liability. This is not to say, however, that foreseeability is indispensable. There are some areas in which the law has established *duties of special care*—often involving dangerous materials—in which the courts may determine that some party caused injuries for which compensation is owed even though those injuries were not in any reasonable sense foreseeable (Appendix II.1.4). And some noteworthy contemporary scholars have even argued that in a number of high-profile tort cases, defendants have been found liable without any causal relation being established between anything they did and the injuries suffered by the plaintiffs.

3.3.3 Analogical Reasoning in the Law: Precedent and *Stare Decisis*

The Extensive Role of Analogies in the Law   To see why legal issues and arguments so often involve analogical reasoning, consider the following scenario. A city ordinance prohibits keeping livestock within the city limits. Clearly people who keep tropical fish, dogs, cats, and parrots are not in violation of this ordinance. But what about someone who keeps geese or chickens? What about a horse? Clearly a herd of cows would be a violation, as would a hog farm, but how about a pig? One pig, say a Vietnamese potbellied pig that spends most of its time indoors, represents a tough case. In some respects a pig is like a cow— it has hooves, is often kept on farms, and so on. But a potbellied pig can also be very much like a dog—truly domesticated, responds to its own name, housebroken, not likely to be eaten by its keeper (certainly not usually intended to be raised for food). So then the issue is whether the pig is more like the cow or the dog in legally relevant respects. If it is more like the cow (in relevant respects), it violates the ordinance; if it is more like the dog, it does not. And settling that requires an argument that mirrors the structure of *analogical reasoning* (section 2.5.3.1), with the purpose of the legal rule against keeping livestock (and allowing pets) playing an important role in determining legal relevance of similarities and differences, as well as providing guidance in weighing those factors.

Analogical reasoning is also widely used in *trial courts* (Appendix II.2.2.2). The *determination of the facts* of the case is the first and (perhaps) most important function of the process of a trial court. In determining facts, courts often employ analogical reasoning on a number of fronts. *Expert testimony,* for example, typically calls for conclusions that are derived on the basis of the expert's past experiences with similar situations. And *circumstantial evidence* is often grounded on common experiences with facts analogous to the present case. Moreover, trial attorneys use analogical arguments in order to persuade the court to apply a certain rule of law to a given set of facts: they construe positive analogies between previous cases that favor their position and the case they are defending, and they use both the direct and the indirect *ways of refutation* (section 2.5.3.3) in order to disarm their opponent's own analogies.

Analogies and the Judicial Decision   In the work of *appellate courts* (Appendix II.2.2.2) and the process of the judicial decision, we find one of the most extensive and important applications of analogical reasoning. Within the Anglo-American system of justice, one major guide for judicial decisions is the *doctrine of precedent.* According to this doctrine, present courts are bound to follow the decisions of courts in prior similar cases. More specifically, the decisions of higher courts in a given jurisdiction set a legally *authoritative* standard for decisions in future cases with *relevantly similar* facts and legal issues in courts at an equal or inferior level within that jurisdiction.

The application of the doctrine of precedent, with its requirement that the law "go on in the same way," involves analogical reasoning par excellence. Since no two cases are alike in every single respect (they surely occur at different times or in different places, if nothing else), the doctrine requires focusing on legally relevant similarities and differences between the current case and authoritative prior cases. Judges *follow precedent* when they determine that a prior case is sufficiently relevantly similar to the present case to require that the two cases be treated in the same (or at least in a relevantly similar) way. Judges *distinguish precedent* when they decide that the present case is sufficiently relevantly dissimilar to the prior case to require that the two cases be treated differently. So precedent requires not only that similar cases be treated similarly, but that dissimilar cases be treated differently.

Stare decisis et non quieta movere is the legal principle that sums up the rationale for the role of precedent in the law. It literally means "let the decision stand and do not disturb what has been settled." *Stare decisis* stipulates that once a court has announced its decision in a case, and arrived at that decision by applying a principle or rule of law to those facts (the "holding," section 4.2.2), judges in future cases are required to adhere to that principle when deciding future cases that are sufficiently similar in legally relevant respects.

The doctrine of *stare decisis* historically arises out of English common law, which relies heavily on case law, that is, the judicial decisions arrived at by judges deciding individual cases (Appendix II.1.1). But there are also powerful theoretical reasons that justify adherence to *stare decisis.* Probably the most important reason is fairness, the cornerstone of justice. As Aristotle pointed out in Book V of his *Nichomachean Ethics,* justice requires that like cases be treated similarly and dissimilar cases be treated differently (in proportion to their dissimilarity). Aristotle's principle seems to represent a formal requirement of both justice and legal reasoning. What the courts should do is treat legally (relevantly) similar cases alike and legally (relevantly) dissimilar cases differently. And this is (arguably) what courts attempt to do, as is most clearly illustrated by how they follow precedent. (Of course, Aristotle's requirement is purely formal in that it does not specify what counts as a legally relevant similarity or difference, nor does it contain a procedure for "weighing" similarities and differences.)

Beyond fairness, reasons cited in support of *stare decisis* include *efficiency* (judges do not have to "start from scratch" every time they confront a new case), *stability* and *predictability* (judges are required to decide cases according to the rule of law, as opposed to their own personal whims and arbitrary beliefs and preferences), *confidence* (the general public respects the workings of the legal system), and *pragmatic necessity* (given the inevitable generality and vagueness of statutory law). All in all, it seems that *stare decisis* can be justified on both pragmatic and principled grounds.

Stare decisis is clearly a very powerful and important legal doctrine, but it is also subject to certain limitations. For one thing, it cannot determine what a court should do if there are conflicting prior decisions, for example, two prior relevantly similar cases that the court appears to be bound to follow, but the decisions lead to conflicting results in the current case. More importantly, although *stare decisis* imposes a general obligation on courts to follow precedent, the fact is that sociopolitical, technological, and historical circumstances change with time. Thus the relevant similarity of previously decided analogous cases is a matter of judicial interpretation and argument, and this means that precedent can be, and often is, overruled. Judges continuously break and reinterpret previous decisions. Nonetheless, though adherence to precedent is not absolutely binding, departure from precedent stands in need of justification: if a departure from established precedent is deemed necessary by particular judge in a case, she is then obligated to provide explicit *reasons* that purportedly *justify* that decision. Consider, for example, how Supreme Court Justices O'Connor, Kennedy, and Souter write with regard to the circumstances that may justify them in overruling precedent:

> Even when the decision to overrule a prior case is not [virtually] foreordained, [the] rule of *stare decisis* is not an "inexorable command." . . . Rather, when this Court reexamines a prior holding, its judgment is customarily informed by a series of prudential and pragmatic considerations designed to test the consistency of overruling a prior decision with the ideal of the rule of law, and to gauge the respective costs of reaffirming and overruling a prior case. Thus, for example, we may ask whether the rule has proved to be intolerable simply in defying practical work-ability; whether the rule is subject to a kind of reliance that would lend a special hardship to the consequences of overruling and add inequity to the cost of repudiation; whether related principles of law have so far developed as to have left the old rule no more than a remnant of abandoned doctrine; or whether facts have so changed or come to be seen so differently, as to have robbed the old rule of significant application or justification . . .
>
> From *Planned Parenthood of Southeastern Pennsylvania v. Casey*,
> 112 S. Ct. 2791 (1992)

Although the language is at times obscure, the justices are acknowledging that *stare decisis* can conflict with other principles that are (at least) equally important within the law, and can even be overruled by them. The duty to follow precedent can be overridden.

3.4 HOW JUDGES REASON

Judicial reasoning, especially that of appellate courts, has been the center of much attention in discussions of legal reasoning. The prominent issues addressed include the importance of appellate judicial decisions in a common law system, the presumably objective character of that decision, and the controversial role of reasoning in reaching that decision.

The *importance* of the judicial decision in a *common law legal system* (Appendix II.1.1) like ours cannot be overemphasized. We have seen that, unlike trial courts that seek to determine the facts of a case, the main function of appellate courts is to settle *points of law* (Appendix II.2.2.2). The decisions of these appellate courts are most important for the *rule of law*, the objective and principled settlement of disputes via the employment of a stable system of laws. These decisions become part of the "settled law" and, under the rule of *stare decisis*, provide both a basis for and a constraint on future judicial decisions. From a lawyer's perspective, moreover, these decisions become the basis of predictions of the ultimate outcome of his case should it get litigated.

An important presupposition that underlies the weight placed on judicial adjudication is that judicial decisions are objective and justifiable. The judicial process, as opposed to the political process involved in selecting legislators and drafting and voting on pieces of legislation, is supposed to be impartial, rational, principled, and based on the application of legal rights and responsibilities that are grounded in the law itself. Alternatively, the traditional view of the judiciary includes the presupposition that courts do not decide cases arbitrarily or on a whim. Instead, courts reach their decisions by employing some principle, rule, or standard that is derived from a legally authoritative source such as legislation or precedent. The courts are supposed to apply these standards in a way that yields decisions that are reasoned, impartial, and consistent from case to case.

That a judicial decision is a *reasoned* decision, that is, one that has been derived according to the rules of logic, seems to be a necessary condition for satisfying the ideal of objectivity. But even this claim turns out to be controversial. Volumes of legal scholarship address such difficult questions as the following: just what *exactly* does the judge do when she decides a case? What kinds of arguments are used? To what extent, if any, is reasoning (as opposed to whim, politics, or even the judge's prejudices) involved in reaching a decision? Is there a distinctive form of judicial reasoning that sets it apart from that performed by ordinary people when they deal with practical affairs? Is the predominant form of judicial reasoning deductive or inductive?

Disagreement on these matters is widespread, and competing theories of adjudication provide sharply contrasted explanations. We provide a brief overview of some central theories of judicial adjudication later in section 3.4.3. In what immediately follows, we highlight some key elements of the debate on which there seems to be a fairly solid consensus. For expository purposes and for the sake of simplicity, we focus on two widely used forms or patterns of judicial reasoning:

- Reasoning from rules
- Reasoning from cases

3.4.1 Reasoning from Statutory Rules

The notion of a "rule" in legal discussion is ambiguous, so let us begin with two clarifications. First, in our discussion, we will understand the notion of legal rule rather broadly to mean "statement of legal requirement(s) in a given set of circumstances." Thus statements like "Driving above 65 miles/hour is prohibited," "Wills require two witnesses to be valid," and "No vehicles are allowed in the city park" are rules in our sense. Second, though rules of law can be judge-made (in a common law system), a large part of the law consists of rules enacted by a legislature or an administrative agency. For simplicity, we will focus here on *statutory* rules enacted by a legislature.

Reasoning from enacted statutory rules is supposed to involve a three-step process. First, the judge identifies some statutory rule that most appropriately applies to the case being decided. Next the judge interprets the rule, ascertaining its intended meaning and scope. Finally, the judge employs the *deductive model* (section 3.2) and applies the rule to the present set of facts. The legal result is the logical product of this arguably mechanical process.

Consider, for example, how this would work when a judge decides a simple case of a person who drives a motorcycle in a park where a posted municipal ordinance reads "No vehicles are allowed in the park." The judge's reasoning begins with the ordinance itself; he does not need to "look for" a prior similar case because the rule clearly and unquestionably applies to riding a motorcycle in the park. Then, with "No vehicles are allowed in the park" as the major premise and the facts of the case as the minor premise of the *syllogism* (section 3.2), deductive reasoning "automatically" yields the conclusion that the motorcyclist violated the ordinance.

As this rather simple illustration shows, the main features of reasoning from statutory rules seem to be these:

- The starting point of reasoning is an enacted, already existing statutory rule.
- The appropriate form of reasoning is the deductive model.
- In most cases, the decision follows from the rule in a quasi-mechanical manner.

There are both advantages and disadvantages associated with judicial reasoning from rules. On the positive side, this pattern of reasoning accommodates best the *commonsense view of the role and function of the judiciary:* in accordance with the doctrine of separation of powers (Appendix II.2.1), the main function of the judiciary is not to make up rules, but rather to apply existing enacted rules of law to specific cases.

On the negative side, however, this model of reasoning tends to oversimplify the complexity of actual judicial decision making and even conceals the highly active role that judges play in shaping the law. To see this, it will suffice to focus on just one aspect of the complexity of judicial reasoning from rules, namely, the difficulties involved in the identification and application of legal rules. There are several problems arising from the alleged "mechanical" application of statutory rules by the judiciary, including *conflicts* of equally applicable rules, and rules so *complex* and confusing that they require judges to do considerable nonmechanical work to ascertain their scope and fit. But the main problem is the *indeterminacy* of rules: even the most apparently simple statutes may be the source of *uncertainty* that can only be resolved through judicial *statutory interpretation.* Indeed, the subject is important enough to require separate treatment.

3.4.1.1 Statutory Uncertainty
A significant part of adjudication is devoted to the *interpretation* of unclear statutes. There are several reasons why statutes give rise to uncertainty and require judicial clarification. We can distinguish at least three closely related *sources of statutory uncertainty:*

- Manner of origin
- Gaps and unanticipated situations
- Indeterminacy due to ambiguities and vagueness in language

Origin   Imprecision and lack of clarity in statutes sometimes is due to the way they come into existence. Statutes are often composed through a team effort by politically minded legislators. The legislative process involves compromise and the accommodation of conflicting interests, wills, and intentions. Consequently, the wording of statutes frequently reflects the motives of the legislators in terms of (a) how the legislation will be seen by constituents, and (b) getting other legislators to vote for the legislation. So often for a bill to pass, it must not be too clear or precise. Some imprecision and lack of clarity is at times inescapable.

Gaps   Statutes are inherently static: they are enacted *before* the actual situations to which they purport to apply have occurred; and once they have been enacted, they remain as is (unless modified by a subsequent statute). Even if legislators always strove for comprehensiveness and kept an eye toward covering the largest possible variety of situations, they are not omniscient, nor can they keep up with the continuous changes in science and technology. The *Sherman Anti-Trust Act,* for example, was enacted in 1890 to combat monopolistic practices that restrain trade and aim at eliminating competition. Yet as the recent dispute between Microsoft and the Justice Department indicates, none of the authors of the Sherman Anti-Trust Act could have anticipated whether bundling a specific web browser (that is, *Explorer*) with a particular computer operating system (that is, *Windows 98*) should be considered a practice that violates the *Sherman Anti-Trust Act.*

Ambiguity and Vagueness   Since ordinary language is vague, and since statutes are written in ordinary language, it would be impossible for legislators to specify every term's exact meaning and scope. So *vagueness* and *ambiguity* (section 1.2.1) cannot be completely eliminated. Granted, some sources of uncertainty can be reduced through the extensive use of *stipulative definitions* (section 1.2.2.2), but it is often up to the court to clarify ambiguities and vagueness encountered in statutes.

3.4.1.2 Statutory Interpretation

Courts engage in statutory interpretation when they attempt to resolve statutory uncertainty. But exactly what are courts doing (and what *should* they be doing) when they "interpret" a statute? Once again, legal scholars do not agree on a single answer. For present purposes, we will ignore a host of complications and focus on two main techniques or approaches to statutory interpretation:

- The textualist approach (focus on text)
- The purposive approach (focus on purpose)

Focus on Text   One approach to statutory interpretation is to hold that the starting point and the main focus ought to be the *text* of the statute. According to this approach, the text "ought to speak for itself," and the words actually used in the statute are to be understood in their *ordinary sense.* Thus *vehicle* in the statute "No vehicles are allowed in the park" should be understood as having its ordinary, everyday meaning, which includes at its core such things as cars and motorcycles (or at any rate, as Justice Holmes argued in *McBoyle,* "things that run on land").

But the textualist approach is not without its problems. For one thing, ordinary meanings by themselves will not resolve hard cases involving ambiguity or vagueness. For example, the ordinary understanding of *vehicle* in "No vehicles are allowed in the park" does not seem helpful in deciding what counts as a vehicle in cases where we are confronted with such things as baby strollers, lawn mowers, wheelchairs, and roller skates. Further, following ordinary language or the "letter" of the text can lead to patently absurd results. Taken literally, "No vehicles are allowed in the park" would seem to prohibit an ambulance from entering the park for an emergency rescue; and as Professor Lon Fuller has observed, a war memorial, which includes a military jeep placed on a pedestal, could not be erected according to the letter of the same rule. There are cases, then, that call for interpretation in light of the spirit or purpose of a statute.

Focus on Purpose   The main tenet of this approach is that the interpretation of statutes ought to be guided by the goal(s) or *purpose(s)* of the statute. Thus, the aim of interpretation, according to this approach, is to discern *legislative intent,* what the legislature intended to achieve by enacting a given statute. The *special* purposes of the statute are always taken into account, but on some variants of the approach, the context and the *general* purposes or goals of the legal system of which a given statute is a part should also be taken into consideration. Discerning legislative intent in a given case may involve consideration of the state of the law before the statute was enacted, as well as the legislative history of the statute including drafts, supporting materials, and floor discussions.

Still, judicial appeals to legislative purpose will always generate controversy. For one thing, some have argued that this approach would actually have judges rewriting legislation according to what they perceive as legislative intent. Not only are judges not appropriately trained or equipped to rewrite legislation, the separation of powers doctrine (Appendix II.2.1) would dictate that this is a legislative, not a judicial, function. Moreover, there is something misleading in referring to *the* intent of the legislature as if it were a single identifiable entity, since legislators act as a team in enacting statutes and the final product is a compromise among many conflicting views. Although one may discern many and various individual intentions among legislators, one cannot discern *the* will of the legislature, for there is no such thing.

Sample Application: Text or Purpose?
Church of the Holy Trinity v. United States,
143 U.S. 457 (1892)

It must be noted that focusing on text and focusing on purpose are not mutually exclusive interpretive approaches. Courts often adopt both models in deciding a case, and the text and purpose of a statute most often dictate the same result. But it is also common for the two approaches to clash in rather dramatic ways. A striking case in point is *Church of the Holy Trinity v. United States.*

The Church of the Holy Trinity, a religious corporation in New York, made a contract with one E. W. Warren, then an alien residing in England, to move to New York and enter into service for the church as its rector and pastor. As part of the contract, the church prepaid Warren's cost of transportation. The church was prosecuted for violation of the Foreign Contract Labor Act of 1885, a federal statute that provided in part:

> It shall be unlawful for any person, company, partnership, or corporation, in any manner whatsoever, to prepay the transportation, or in any way assist or encourage the importation or migration of any alien or aliens, any foreigner or foreigners, into the United States . . . to perform labor or service of any kind in the United States . . . .

A strict and literal interpretation of the text seems to indicate clearly that the church violated the statute. The text clearly and unambiguously prohibits the prepaid transportation of aliens entering the United States under a labor contract with a U.S. corporation; the Church of Holy Trinity had a contract with the alien Pastor Warren, and prepaid the transportation of this alien to come to the U.S. so he could work as a pastor. A simple application of deductive reasoning would then yield that the church had violated the statute. Indeed, the lower court reasoned exactly in this manner, and ruled against the church.

Interestingly enough, when the case reached the Supreme Court, the decision of the lower court was reversed. The Court admitted that the ordinary meanings of the words of the statute—the literal interpretation of the *text*—supported the decision of the lower court. Nonetheless, the spirit or *purpose* of the statute, the Supreme Court reasoned, called for a reversal. In delivering the opinion of the Court, Justice Brewer focused on the purpose of the statute and interpreted it in light of what he perceived to be the legislature's intent in enacting the statute. He argued that Congress intended to put an end to the then widespread practice of corporations prepaying the passage of "great numbers of an ignorant and servile class of foreign laborers" to work cheaply under contract for a number of years. The importation of cheap immigrant *laborers*—and specifically *manual laborers,* as the legislative history indicated—Justice Brewer argued, was the "evil to be remedied" by the enactment of the Foreign Contract Labor Act. It was never the intention of the legislature, Justice Brewer reasoned, to include pastors and other "brain toilers" in the class of "cheap immigrant labor." In view of the purpose of the statute, the Court concluded that the Church of the Holy Trinity was not in violation of the Foreign Contract Labor Act after all.

> ### Canons of Statutory Construction
>
> A common, though controversial, tool of statutory interpretation is the employment of the so-called *canons of construction.* These are interpretive rules of thumb invoked by judges in the process of judicial interpretation of statutes, and they can be either "linguistic" or "substantive." An example of the former type is the *ejusdem generis* canon according to which general language following a list of specific items should be interpreted in light of those specific items. (Notice how this applies in the *McBoyle* case!) On the other hand, the principle "no person should benefit from his own wrongdoing" that we will encounter in *Riggs v. Palmer* (section 5.1) is an example of a substantive canon with a great deal of content.

3.4.1.3 A Note on Constitutional Interpretation

The Constitution of the United States enjoys a most special status in our system. For one thing, it sets the foundations of our democratic form of government by incorporating a system of checks and balances that gives expression to the ideals of the *separation of powers doctrine, federalism, and civil liberties* (Appendix II.2.1). For another thing, it establishes its own supremacy as the ultimate law of the land, a law that takes precedence over any other law, federal or state (Article VI).

Given the paramount importance of the Constitution, it should not be surprising that issues of constitutional interpretation engender highly complex and controversial debates. That the Constitution is often in need of interpretation is an obvious matter (think, for example, of such concepts as *due process of law* and *freedom of speech* that are to be found in it). But who should be the final authority in interpreting it? And what is to count as the correct interpretation?

Neither of these questions has an easy answer. Thus, for example, with regard to the issue of the ultimate saying in the interpretation of the Constitution, there is widespread agreement that it belongs to the Supreme Court. Yet critics have pointed out that *judicial review* (the power to interpret the constitutionality of laws as well as the "true" meaning of the Constitution) is fundamentally antidemocratic. The issue of the correct interpretation, on the other hand, is even more controversial. The rift between textual and intentional (purposive) interpretation that we just encountered with statutes spills over into the interpretation of the Constitution. But there is an additional layer of complexity: some theorists claim that both the textualist and the purposive approach share a common fault when applied to the Constitution. Namely, both approaches go back to the framers and seek to understand the *original understanding* of the framers (*originalism*) or seek to *interpret* either the meaning of the language used in the original text or the intentions of those who wrote it (*interpretivism*). Yet both approaches are wrong, the critics claim. The correct alternative ought to be *nonoriginalism* (or *noninterpretivism*), the approach that construes the Constitution as a dynamic, flexible document that evolves with time and adjusts to the sociopolitical reality of the present and the immediate future.

3.4.2 Reasoning from Cases

Reasoning from rules is not the only way judges adjudicate. In a common law system like ours, the major form of judicial reasoning is arguably not from rules but rather *from previously adjudicated cases.* The pattern of reasoning from cases, or *reasoning by example,* is described by Professor Edward Levi as follows:

> It is a three-step process described by the doctrine of precedent in which a proposition descriptive of the first case is made into a rule of law and then applied to the next similar situation. The steps are these: similarity is seen between cases; next the rule of law inherent in the first case is announced; then the rule of law is made applicable in the second case.
>
> *An Introduction to Legal Reasoning,* The University of Chicago Press, Chicago, 1949, pp. 1–2

If the "Levi-three-step" is right, reasoning from case to case seems to work as follows: The judge starts by comparing the case at hand with an apparently similar previously adjudicated case. The judge determines whether the present case is sufficiently relevantly similar to the (prior) controlling case to justify treating this case in the way the prior case was treated, or whether this case is sufficiently relevantly dissimilar to require treating them differently. (Once again, the presupposition is that judges are trained to identify controlling precedents and to employ the law's criteria of relevant similarity and dissimilarity in an objective, reasoned way. But both the choice of the appropriate prior case and the determination of relevant similarity and difference between cases are controversial.) Once the judge has decided that precedent must be followed, she extricates the rule of the precedent case and then applies that rule of law to the present case.

As opposed to reasoning from rules, the main features of reasoning from cases appear, thus, to be these:

- The starting point of reasoning is a previously decided case.
- The predominant form of reasoning is inductive, analogical reasoning.
- The judge has to make difficult determinations of relevant similarities and differences between cases. It is up to the judge to decide which precedent is the controlling one, and whether precedent needs to be followed, distinguished, or (in a higher court) overruled.

Sample Application: *MacPherson v. Buick*

To see how the features of reasoning from cases work in practice, let us look at a case dealing with the issue of liability of manufacturers to persons other than the immediate purchaser, namely, the often-cited case of *MacPherson v. Buick,* 217 N.Y. (1916).

While MacPherson was traveling at low speed in his Buick, a defective rear wheel suddenly collapsed and sent his car into a ditch. MacPherson was injured and sued the manufacturer, Buick Motor Company (but not the dealer from whom he had purchased the car—Buick sold the car to the dealer who in turn sold it to MacPherson). The trial court found for the plaintiff (MacPherson), and a subsequent appeals court affirmed the judgment of the lower trial court. The case reached the New York Court of Appeals, which, through Judge Cardozo, affirmed the judgment of the lower appeals court.

To see how Justice Cardozo reasoned his way to this conclusion, we should notice first that *MacPherson* is a classic example of case law; statutes played no role in the decision, and prior relevantly similar cases were crucial. Prior cases had established that manufacturers were not liable to third parties who were injured by negligently manufactured items *except* when the item was "inherently dangerous." Two cases were especially important to the decision in *MacPherson.* Perhaps the closest precedent case was *Winterbottam v. Wright,* 10 Meeson & Welsby 109 (1842), a British case that American courts followed, in which recovery was not allowed when the wheel of a horse-drawn carriage collapsed, resulting in serious injuries to its driver (who was not the purchaser). The "inherently dangerous" provision itself arose out of the decision in *Thomas v. Winchester,* 6 N.Y. 397 (1852). In that case, belladonna (poison) was erroneously labeled as extract of dandelion by one of the manufacturer's employees. A pharmacist bought the belladonna from Winchester (the manufacturer) and sold it to Thomas (the third party), whose wife became sick when she used it. Thomas sued the manufacturer, not the pharmacist, and the court ruled that he was entitled to recover because the poison was inherently dangerous.

In the time between *Thomas* and *MacPherson,* courts applied the "inherently dangerous" rule to third-party liability cases and determined that the inherently dangerous category included not only poisons (from *Thomas*), but gunpowder, torpedoes, and locomotives as well. Things outside the inherently dangerous category included pictures, tables, chairs, and horse-drawn carriages (from *Winterbottam*). The central issue in *MacPherson* thus becomes into which category to place the Buick. The appellant (Buick Company) insisted that an automobile is not like poison, a torpedo, or any other standard exemplar of the "inherently dangerous" category and thus does not belong in the category of inherently dangerous items. The plaintiff (MacPherson), on the other hand, argued that given the way automobiles are propelled by explosive gases, they are more similar to locomotives than wagons, and they are thus inherently dangerous items.

In deciding *MacPherson v. Buick,* Judge Cardozo determined that the controlling precedent of a manufacturer's liability to a third party was to be found in *Thomas.* Of course, the manufacturer's liability to a third party in *Thomas* involved a poison, an item that clearly falls into the "inherently dangerous" category, while *MacPherson* involved an automobile, an item that may not clearly fall into that category. Thus, by the rules of analogical reasoning, it would seem that *MacPherson* should be *distinguished* from *Thomas.* So why did Judge Cardozo *follow* Thomas instead? The answer is that Judge Cardozo reasoned that courts after *Thomas* had generally construed "inherently dangerous" in a narrow fashion. But the proper understanding of the "inherently dangerous" rule, Judge Cardozo argued, calls for the adoption of a more *extended* meaning of the rule as follows: "If the nature of a thing is such that it is reasonably certain to place life and limb in peril when negligently made, it is then a thing of danger. Its nature gives warning of the consequences to be expected. If to the element of danger there is added knowledge that the thing will be used by persons other than the purchaser, and used without new tests, then, irrespective of contract, the manufacturer of this thing of danger is under a duty to make it carefully." Moreover, Cardozo clarified, "there must be knowledge of a danger not merely possible but probable." It follows that, as long as it is known that an item is *probably* dangerous if defective, the manufacturer of that item may be found liable for negligence to a third party.

When we understand the rule this way, it becomes clear that the Buick is more like the locomotive in relevant ways than it is like the horse-drawn carriage. Among the factors that make it so are the requirement of a license to operate both the Buick and the locomotive, and the fact that each is propelled by explosive gases and able to travel at high speeds. So the Buick is inherently dangerous after all, and the manufacturer must compensate MacPherson for his injuries.

3.4.3 The Nature and Legitimacy of Judicial Adjudication

The acceptance of the doctrine of the separation of powers (Appendix II.2.1) necessitates that the function of the judiciary be distinct from that of the legislature. If powers are truly to be kept separate, the judges cannot be "legislating from the bench," whether explicitly or covertly. But then the doctrine seems to presuppose a theory of judicial decision making, and indeed, a rather specific theory at that. What is needed is a blueprint for how judges can apply a valid law, which originates in the legislative branch, to a set of facts and arrive at a legal conclusion without in any way co-opting the law-making function. Now the commonsense view seems to support this role for the judiciary—the popular press and politicians are awash with claims that we need judges who do not themselves make law, but who simply apply the law. So just what are judges supposed to be doing? Here are some main answers to this question.

3.4.3.1 Formalism and Rule-Scepticism

Perhaps the most intuitively plausible, and hence popular, answer to this question of how judges adjudicate lies within the view known as *legal formalism.* According to this view, judges apply legal rules that are of "extrajudicial origin," and these rules are "definite, detailed provisions for definite, detailed states of fact." The judicial function would then be distinct from the legislative, since the rules that judges apply come from outside the judiciary and are specific enough that they neither require nor permit any "creativity" on the part of the judge who is applying them. The application of legal rules is a *mechanical process* in which the judge is adept at analyzing factual situations, has a command of the mass of valid laws within the legal system, and then simply "fits the rule" to the case at hand; the legal decision follows automatically from this process. So the formalist would say that properly constructed legal rules would maintain the separation of powers by allowing judges no room for creatively "legislating from the bench," since the proper application of these rules automatically dictates the correct legal result. And so in theory, it should not matter which judge is applying the rules—relevantly similar cases will yield relevantly similar results. In this way laws will be made in the legislature and merely applied by the judiciary.

But as you might expect, not everyone agrees with the formalists. A number of critics of formalism have produced arguments designed to show that what judges actually do in deciding cases is significantly different from what the formalists claim judges are (or "should be") doing. Some of these critics of formalism are proponents of *rule-scepticism,* a view that is sceptical that rules and their application by judges are as the formalist would like us to believe. A well-known example borrowed from H.L.A. Hart shows how a rule-sceptic might try to undercut formalism. Let us assume that "No motor vehicles are permitted in Central Park on weekends" is a valid law in New York City, so that it was appropriately introduced in and passed by the city council. Suppose it has survived various appeals and is now firmly entrenched within the city's legal system. Let us assume that police have been patrolling the park, and that (predictably) semi-truck drivers are cited and toddlers on tricycles are not. Now here is the problem. What about someone riding a moped? Someone in a motorized wheelchair or in an electrically powered inflatable raft? A child with a toy radio-controlled boat on the duck pond? What about a helicopter hovering above the Tavern on the Green? Someone in a hovercraft? A guy with a gasoline-powered, radio-controlled B-36? An ambulance? The point should be obvious—"No motor vehicles in the park" seems to pose at least two difficulties for the formalist. First, it appears that the definitions of what counts as a "motor vehicle" and as being "in the park" crucially affect the application of this rule. Second, different judges could clearly claim to be "applying" this rule to the same case (say, the moped) and arrive at different legal conclusions. Since the application by judges of rules within a legal system seems to mirror in important ways the "no motor vehicles in the park" case, formalism seems to be dead wrong. But if we have to abandon formalism, what hope is there for the actual separation of powers?

3.4.3.2 Legal Realism and Critical Legal Studies

The great positivist H.L.A. Hart has attempted to account for the legitimate claims of rule-scepticism within a positivist framework, and Ronald Dworkin has used some of the rule-sceptics' points in developing his view, which shares some features with traditional legal naturalism. But neither has bought into the rule-sceptic's arguments wholeheartedly. On the other hand, two camps in legal theory have fully embraced rule-scepticism, and to them we now turn.

The American *legal realists* have argued that legal theory needs to be more "realistic" about just what lies behind judges' decisions, as well as the nature of the law itself. The typical realist argument begins with the recommendation that we adopt a particular point of view in conducting our analysis of legal systems, since the choice of one's point of view influences how the law will appear to us. Oliver Wendell Holmes remarked that the law looks very different to the good man as opposed to the evil man, and argued that the proper point of view for legal theory to adopt is that of either a person consulting her attorney or an attorney advising her client. From that point of view, the realists argue, what matters is *how the courts will in fact rule* on the matter that concerns the client—the issue is how the actions of the judiciary will affect the client should she pursue a certain course of action. And from that point of view, the decisions of the courts are of paramount importance, which has led some realists to argue that *the law is what the judge (or courts) say it is,* as opposed to the abstract principles of the naturalist or the "proper origins" test of the positivist.

Further, the realist advises us to look at the actual decisions of courts as guides for conducting our inquiry into the nature of law. Indeed, that is what the responsible attorney would do prior to advising her client. And when we do look at this "settled law" (past decisions of courts), we see that the idea that there are rules and principles that determine the outcome in all cases is a myth. Instead, we find unclear rules, gaps in the rules, and rules that conflict with each other. What actually determines the outcome is the judge's beliefs and attitudes toward a particular type of case. Legal history also shows that in most cases, the judge is not legally bound to reach any particular legal conclusion; and in difficult cases, it seems entirely up to the judge as to which way a decision should go. The realist thus argues that what we call legal rules are at best simply *predictions* of how judges might decide future relevantly similar cases. And since legal rules that determine legal outcomes—and are of extrajudicial origin—are out the window, so is the doctrine of separation of powers, which some have referred to as a "pious little fiction." So the realists are rule-sceptics with a vengeance—they are sceptical about the existence of any workable legal rules at all.

A similar albeit more radical espousal of scepticism can be found in the views of the *critical legal studies (CLS)* movement. Some proponents of this view have been influenced by Marxist political theory; they argue that the law is not a set of rules or principles as much as it is an instrument employed by those who are well-off and have power to hold onto their position and to keep others "in their place." The central tenet of CLS is that rules and principles, which lie at the core of traditional accounts of valid law, are *indeterminate* in that they do not demand that judges reach one and only one legally correct result when deciding a case. When we look at the settled law (as the realists also suggest), we see not a unified system of clear rules, but instead *a "patchwork quilt" of internal contradictions and inconsistencies.* What this means is that anything goes: a modern legal system is like a "shopping list" or "menu" of laws reflecting a variety of conflicting political ideologies and a judge can find some justification for what counts as "the law" for any decision that she wants to hand down in any particular case. Thus, the temperament and political ideology of the judge, rather than a set of clear rules, determines how a case gets decided; and those who have power and privilege are careful to pick as judges those persons whose political (and other) leanings are favorable to their interests. So cases get decided on the basis of politics and ideology rather than impartial application of rules and principles. Any other picture of legal validity is a gross distortion designed to perpetuate a set of myths about legal reality that are convenient and serve to legitimate the power structure that is in place.

3.4.4 Concluding Remarks on Judicial Reasoning

We can now identify two closely related characteristics of judicial reasoning, which we point out without much elaboration. First, judicial reasoning is a complex enterprise that departs from ordinary reasoning in some ways. Second, the idiosyncratic character of judicial reasoning raises serious questions about the role of the judges and the legitimacy of the judicial decision.

At first glance one may doubt whether there is anything in judicial reasoning that distinguishes it from "good-old-fashioned logic." A closer look, however, reveals that judicial reasoning includes, but is not exhausted by, formal logic. Despite the obvious overlap between formal logic and judicial reasoning, there are important differences as well. One major difference between logic and judicial reasoning is this: even if a judge believes that a prior decision was incorrect, the rule of *stare decisis* creates a *duty* for the judge to follow it nonetheless. In logic, by contrast, once a mistake is exposed, there is no duty whatsoever to acknowledge its authority, let alone follow it. Another point to note is that when a court's decision establishes a precedent, logic alone will not determine exactly what precedent it establishes, yet courts *must* determine what that precedent requires in applying it to the case before them. Nor can logic tell us when two parties are in legally relevantly similar circumstances. To be sure, the *method* of reasoning from case to case is formally guided by the pattern of analogical reasoning. But the important *judgment* of the relevant similarities and differences between two cases is not a matter that can be spelled out by logic alone. Finally, it should be obvious from our discussion of statutory interpretation that the all-important enterprise of interpreting statutes does not, and cannot, follow any predetermined pattern dictated by logic. Indeed, judges have considerable flexibility in employing resources beyond mere logic in order to interpret the law and reach a decision. This brings us to the second important issue raised by judicial reasoning, the issue of the legitimacy of the judicial activity.

The commonsense, ordinary citizen's view of judicial reasoning construes it as a fairly "mechanical" production of outcomes from preexisting rules of law. But we have seen that the enterprise of applying the law to specific disputes is far from a mechanical process. From interpreting statutes to judging similarities and differences among cases, every step of judicial reasoning in particular and of adjudication in general involves the judge in highly complex decision-making procedures that require considerable flexibility and discretion. But here is exactly where the problem lies: though in theory the judiciary is supposed to apply laws enacted by the legislature, in practice judges possess and exercise considerable power to shape the law as they see fit. But given the separation of powers doctrine (Appendix II.2.1), this raises important questions about the legitimacy of the judicial function.

PART III

CASE ANALYSIS

CHAPTER 4

GUIDELINES FOR ANALYZING CASES

4.1 THE WRITTEN OPINION

Appellate courts, unlike trial courts, often publish a *written opinion* when deciding a case. This written opinion should not be thought of as a description of a judge's actual psychological process, but rather as an attempt to *justify* the decision reached in the case. Thus, an appellate opinion is a highly argumentative text loaded with legal reasons and arguments that are provided in support of the judge's decision (that is, *why* the judge decided the case the way she did). As such, each opinion is a paradigm of judicial reasoning and a potential learning tool. Indeed, in law school, the analysis of appellate opinions ("case method") is the prominent pedagogical model for teaching legal reasoning.

A written opinion usually follows a standard format. The judge sets out the legally relevant facts of the case (key facts), identifies the legal issue(s) raised by the facts, provides the legal reasoning supporting the decision, and announces either that he agrees with the decision of the lower court (judgment *affirmed*) or that he disagrees (judgment *reversed*). Of course, the "heart" of the opinion is the judge's reasoning involved in support of his decision. And we have already seen (section 3.4) that this is a complex enterprise involving such difficult tasks as surveying prior cases containing similar facts and issues; identifying which (if any) statutes, rules, or principles of prior cases have a bearing on the case; making judgments about the relevancy of the legal "authorities" considered; selecting the applicable rule of law and incorporating the rule into a holding; "fitting" the elements of that rule to the facts of the case; and inferring a legal conclusion that addresses the legal issue raised by the case.

Occasionally an appeals court will issue a judgment containing only one opinion, which represents the judgment of the entire court, but often an appeals court will publish more than one opinion in a case. Most often there will be two opinions: a *majority opinion,* which contains the legal decision of the court and the arguments for it agreed upon by a majority of the court, and a *dissenting opinion,* which contains arguments purporting to show that the majority reached the incorrect conclusion in the case. But things can get very complicated. Some cases include, in addition to the court's majority opinion, what are called *separate concurring opinions,* in which the authors sometimes argue that the court reached the correct conclusion but disagree with the reasoning offered in support of the conclusion. A concurring opinion might agree with the conclusion of the court and even agree with a portion of the court's reasoning, but disagree with other aspects of that reasoning. Likewise, there can be more than one dissenting opinion (at the U.S. Supreme Court, four would appear to be the limit) containing separate arguments for why the court's resolution of the case is incorrect.

4.2 The Elements of a Written Opinion

The old saying "different strokes for different folks" perfectly describes approaches toward reading an appellate written opinion. Different people have different purposes in mind, and those different purposes suggest different strategies. Thus, for example, legal practitioners need to know how to "brief" a case, that is, how to present a written summary of the legally important elements of a judicial opinion. And this involves several tasks that go beyond the extrication of the arguments judges provide to justify their decision (that is, the reasoning in the case). To stay within our goals in this book, in what follows, we confine ourselves to a quick synopsis of the briefing of elements other than the reasoning involved in a particular case.

4.2.1 Secondary Elements

In briefing a case, legal researchers need to identify several of its "minor" elements, elements that include (but are not limited to) such items as the following:

- **Title of case (caption) and official citation:** For example, we may see the following:

    Furman v. Georgia

    408 U.S. 238 (1972)

    This tells us that the case is reported in volume 408 of the *United States Reports* (the official record of the cases decided by the Supreme Court) beginning on page 238, and that the case was decided in 1972.

- **Synopses or headnotes:** These are brief summaries of issues decided in the case. Notice that these summaries are not part of the court's opinion; they are editor-made and not part of the actual case. For example, in the beginning of *Riggs* we find:

    Rights of Legatees—Murder of Testator

    The law of New York relating to the probate of wills and the distributions of estates will not be construed so as to secure the benefit of a will to a legatee who has killed the testator in order to prevent a revocation of the will. GRAY and DANFORTH, JJ., dissenting.

- **Procedural history/parties' attorneys:** Thus, in *Riggs* we find:

  > Appeal from supreme court, general term, third department.
  >
  > Leslie W. Russell, for appellants. W. M. Hawkins for respondents.

- **The judge who delivers (authors) the opinion of the court:** For example, in the beginning of *McBoyle v. United States* we find:

  > *Mr. Justice Holmes delivered the opinion of the Court.*

  This identifies the judge who delivered the majority opinion.

- **The decision of the court:** This is the outcome of the case as captured in the final judgment of the court. This is stated in the end of the case, usually briefly (for example, "Judgment reversed").

4.2.2 Key Elements: Facts, Issue, and Holding

The most crucial element of case-to-case reasoning is the identification of the legal rule of the precedent case, the so-called *holding* of the prior case. But since the holding of a case is supposed to be the answer to the *issue* of the case, which in turn is supposed to incorporate the *facts* of the case, we need to take a step back and examine things in reverse order.

The Facts   The facts of the case constitute the legal "story" of the actual events that led to the controversy at hand. In extricating the legally relevant facts ("key" or "material" facts), one must identify the disputing parties (the *plaintiff* and the *defendant*), their roles in the case (that is, the what-happened-to-whom-and-when of the case), and the plaintiff's legal claim against the defendant (that is, the *cause-of-action* in the case). Extricating key facts is more difficult than it may at first seem. But appeals court judges often provide us with a clear, concise statement early in their opinion; for example, in *Riggs v. Palmer,* 115 N.Y. 506 (1889), they stated:

> On the 13th day of August 1880, Francis B. Palmer made his last will and testament, in which he gave small legacies to his two daughters, Mrs. Riggs and Mrs. Preston, the plaintiffs in this action, and the remainder of his estate to his grandson, the defendant Elmer E. Palmer. . . . At the date of the will, and subsequently to the death of the testator, Elmer lived with him as a member of his family, and at his death was 16 years old. He knew of the provisions made in his favor in the will, and, that he might prevent his grandfather from revoking such provisions, which he had manifested some intention to do, and to obtain the speedy enjoyment and immediate possession of his property, he willfully murdered him by poisoning him. He now claims the property, and the sole question for our determination is, can he have it?

The Issue (in Controversy)   A statement of the issue involves the identification of the legal question (or questions) in dispute. When law students learn to identify the issue(s) of a case, they learn that, ideally, a proper statement of the issue should incorporate the legal question raised by the case and the facts that relate directly to the legal question. Moreover, again ideally, the statement of the issue should be both (i) narrow enough to cover the particular dispute before the court, and (ii) expressed in such a way that the legal question could be answered with a simple "yes" or "no." Thus, for example, a good expression of the issue in *Riggs* would be as follows:

> Do the laws of New York relating to the probate of wills and distribution of estates allow one who has murdered the testator in order to prevent a revocation of the testator's will to inherit property under that will?

It is crucial to note that the identification and formulation of the legal issue in dispute is a most difficult enterprise. The problem is that a proper statement of the issue must "flow from the facts"; that is, it must incorporate the key facts in its formulation. But facts do not lend themselves to a unique interpretation; and thus the facts of a case may be stated *narrowly,* or they may be stated *broadly.* Notice that a broad description of the facts is "just as true" as a narrow description of the facts, since there is no uniquely correct statement of the facts of a case. To be sure, the common law principle of adjudication that calls for judges to decide *only the case before the court* compels us to strive toward a specific construction of the facts and a *narrow framing* of the issues. Nonetheless, for the reasons just mentioned, this ideal is not always easy to achieve.

The Holding   *This is the answer to the issue in controversy, and the law of the case at hand.* In theory, identifying the holding (sometimes referred to as the *ratio decidendi*) should be easy enough once we have identified the issue. In essence, all we need to do now in order to express the holding is to *"restate" the issue in terms of a declarative statement* that accords with the court's verdict. For example, given the way we identified the issue in *Riggs,* we can now state the holding of the case (what the court held in the case) as follows:

> The laws of New York relating to the probate of wills and distribution of estates do not allow one who has murdered the testator in order to prevent a revocation of the testator's will to inherit property under that will.

We can now see why the identification of the holding of a case has been viewed as a crucial task for case-to-case reasoning in common law adjudication. The holding is supposed to capture what the court sees as essential for deciding the particular case at hand, and it is supposed to be *exactly what triggers the application of* stare decisis *for future cases with similar facts.* Thus, the holding of a case controls future cases. When we have a new holding, we have new law (that is, we have judge-made law) that future courts are bound to follow. Still, even though it is technically "new" law, the holding of a case nearly always affirms an existing principle or rule of law.

Given that the holding is the court's answer to the issue in controversy, the "proper" formulation of the holding raises problems similar to those found in formulating the issue, namely, the problem of factual indeterminacy. We have seen that the facts may be overstated or understated, expressed narrowly or expressed broadly. There is no correct formula for stating the issue, and thus there is no ideal formulation of the holding either.

Holding or Dicta?

In theory, the holding is the only element in a judicial opinion that has a direct, binding legal effect. Everything else in the opinion is called *dicta* (or *obiter dicta*) and is supposed to be nonessential to the decision. *Dicta* are judicial utterances that are incidental to the opinion and have no direct bearing on the case before the court. Thus, although judges are required by *stare decisis* to follow the holding of a controlling case, they may choose to be influenced by (or not to be influenced by) the dicta. This is fine in theory, but practice has shown that nothing that is stated in the course of an opinion should be casually dismissed as an item of minor importance. At least if legal sceptics such as the proponents of *legal realism* and *critical legal studies* (section 3.4.3.2) are right, there is no genuine distinction between holding and dicta; the alleged distinction is a myth, and a judge in a subsequent case is always free to introduce his own understanding of what is to count as essential in a precedent. Thus, if the sceptics are right, it is possible for two different judges to agree about the relevance of a given precedent, agree that that precedent should be followed in this case, but disagree about what it means to follow it, since they hold different views on what is the *holding* and what is the *dicta* of that precedent. So they could reach totally opposite legal conclusions based on application of the same precedent!

4.2.3 The Main Focus: The Reasoning Involved

Given the goals of this book, our analysis of cases focuses sharply on the *reasoning* involved in a particular written opinion. We must be clear from the start, nonetheless, that there is both good and bad news here. On the positive side, reading an appellate written opinion with an eye for the reasoning involved in support of the judge's decision is a very good way to learn how to read complex argumentative passages for the arguments involved in them, and an excellent way to acquaint oneself with judicial reasoning. But, on the negative side, we must caution you that judicial reasoning is complex by nature, and the exposition of it in judicial written opinions is not always clear (it is not the job of judges to make sure that their reasoning is easily understood by neophytes in legal reasoning). Thus, you should expect that *you will need to read a case several times* before you begin to analyze it. Moreover, keep in mind that there is no single method for pinpointing what a particular court views as *the* important reason(s) and arguments for its decision. You will have to decide these issues for yourselves, keeping in mind that the arguments given for the court's decision draw from a vast repertoire of divergent criteria. These include the following:

- Statutes
- Past cases
- Writings of legal authorities
- Foreign laws and customs
- General legal rules and principles
- Moral principles
- Considerations of sociopolitical utility
- Claims of legal policy
- Pragmatic considerations
- Rules of logic
- Common sense
- Presumably self-evident truths

TO THINK ABOUT

In *Gregg v. Georgia,* 428 U.S. 153 (1976), the Supreme Court held that "the death penalty is not a form of punishment that may never be imposed, regardless of the circumstances of the offense, regardless of the character of the offender, and regardless of the procedure followed in reaching the decision to impose it. . . ." In the excerpt of the Court's opinion that follows, find and classify the arguments provided in support of the Court's holding.

> The imposition of the death penalty for the crime of murder has a long history of acceptance both in the United States and in England. . . . It is apparent from the text of the Constitution itself that the existence of capital punishment was accepted by the Framers. At the time the Eighth Amendment was ratified, capital punishment was a common sanction in every State. Indeed, the First Congress of the United States enacted legislation providing death as the penalty for specified crimes. . . . The Fifth Amendment, adopted at the same time as the Eighth, contemplated the continued existence of the capital sanction by imposing certain limits on the prosecution of capital cases. . . . And the Fourteenth Amendment, adopted over three-quarters of a century later, similarly contemplates the existence of the capital sanction in providing that no State shall deprive any person of "life, liberty, or property" without due process of law.

> For nearly two centuries, this Court, repeatedly and often expressly, has recognized that capital punishment is not invalid *per se.* . . .

> Four years ago, the petitioners in *Furman* and its companion cases predicated their argument primarily upon the asserted proposition that standards of decency had evolved to the point where capital punishment no longer could be tolerated. . . . The petitioners in the capital cases before the Court today renew the "standards of decency" argument, but developments during the four years since *Furman* have undercut substantially the assumptions upon which their argument rested. Despite the continuing debate, dating back to the nineteenth century, over the morality and utility of capital punishment, it is now evident that a large proportion of American society continued to regard it as an appropriate and necessary criminal sanction.

The most marked indication of society's endorsement of the death penalty for murder is the legislative response to *Furman.* The legislatures of at least 35 States have enacted new statutes that provide for the death penalty for at least some crimes that result in the death of another person. And the Congress of the United States, in 1974, enacted a statute providing the death penalty for aircraft piracy that results in death. . . .

The jury also is a significant and reliable objective index of contemporary values because it is so directly involved. . . . It may be true that evolving standards have influenced juries in recent decades to be more discriminating in imposing the sentence of death. But the relative infrequency of jury verdicts imposing the death sentence does not indicate rejection of capital punishment *per se.* Rather, the reluctance of juries in many cases to impose the sentence may well reflect the humane feeling that this most irrevocable of sanctions should be reserved for a small number of extreme cases. . . . Indeed, the actions of juries in many States since *Furman* are fully compatible with the legislative judgments, reflected in the new statutes, as to the continued utility and necessity of capital punishment in appropriate cases. At the close of 1974 at least 254 persons had been sentenced to death since *Furman,* and by the end of March 1976, more than 460 persons were subject to death sentences. . . .

The death penalty is said to serve two principal social purposes: retribution and deterrence of capital crimes by prospective offenders. In part, capital punishment is an expression of society's moral outrage at particularly offensive conduct. This function may be unappealing to many, but it is essential in an ordered society that asks its citizens to rely on legal processes rather than self-help to vindicate their wrongs. . . ." Retribution is no longer the dominant objective of the criminal law," Williams v. New York, 337 U.S. 241, 248 (1949), but neither is it a forbidden objective nor one inconsistent with our respect for the dignity of men. . . . Indeed, the decision that capital punishment may be the appropriate sanction in extreme cases is an expression of the community's belief that certain crimes are themselves so grievous an affront to humanity that the only adequate response may be the penalty of death.

Statistical attempts to evaluate the worth of the death penalty as a deterrent to crimes by potential offenders have occasioned a great deal of debate. The results simply have been inconclusive. . . . Although some of the studies suggest that the death penalty may not function as a significantly greater deterrent than lesser penalties, there is no convincing empirical evidence either supporting or refuting this view. We may nevertheless assume safely that there are murderers, such as those who act in passion, for whom the threat of death has little or no deterrent effect. But for many others, the death penalty undoubtedly is a significant deterrent. . . . The value of capital punishment as a deterrent of crime is a complex factual issue the resolution of which properly rests with the legislatures, which can evaluate the results of statistical studies in terms of their own local conditions and with a flexibility of approach that is not available to the court. . . . Indeed, many of the post-*Furman* statutes reflect just such a responsible effort to define those crimes and those criminals for which capital punishment is most probably an effective deterrent.

In sum, we cannot say that the judgment of the Georgia legislature that capital punishment may be necessary in some cases is clearly wrong.

In the next chapter, we examine closely two cases, *Riggs v. Palmer* and *Palsgraf v. The Long Island Railroad Co.* These cases, in our opinion, are of average and high difficulty, respectively, and constitute good hands-on examples of a variety of matters in legal reasoning we have touched on in this book.

CHAPTER 5

ANALYZING CASES

Note   For the convenience of the reader, we have edited the original text and numbered it for easy reference. In our analysis of the cases, numbers in bold and in brackets refer to the (edited) text of the cases, and, as always, references inside parentheses following a concept refer to prior sections or appendices of this book.

5.1 *RIGGS V. PALMER*

RIGGS V. PALMER
Court of Appeals of New York
115 N.Y. 506, 22 N.E. 188 (1889)

Rights of Legatees—Murder of Testator

The law of New York relating to the probate of wills and the distributions of estates will not be construed so as to secure the benefit of a will to a legatee who has killed the testator in order to prevent a revocation of the will. GRAY and DANFORTH, JJ., dissenting.

Appeal from supreme court, general term, third department.
Leslie W. Russell, for appellants. *W. M. Hawkins* for respondents.

EARL, J.
    {A}   [1] On the 13th day of August 1880, Francis B. Palmer made his last will and testament, in which he gave small legacies to his two daughters, Mrs. Riggs and Mrs. Preston, the plaintiffs in this action, and the remainder of his estate to his grandson, the defendant Elmer E. Palmer, subject to the support of Susan Palmer, his mother, with a gift over to the two daughters, subject to the support of Mrs. Palmer in case Elmer should survive him and die under age, unmarried, and without any issue. . . . [2] At the date of the will, and subsequently to the death of the testator, Elmer lived with him as a member of his

family, and at his death was 16 years old. [3] He knew of the provisions made in his favor in the will, and, that he might prevent his grandfather from revoking such provisions, which he had manifested some intention to do, and to obtain the speedy enjoyment and immediate possession of his property, he willfully murdered him by poisoning him. [4] He now claims the property, and the sole question for our determination is, can he have it?

{B}   [1] The defendants say that the testator is dead; that his will was made in due form, and has been admitted to probate; and that therefore it must have effect according to the letter of the law. [2] It is quite true that statutes regulating the making, proof, and effect of wills and the devolution of property, if literally construed, and if their force and effect can in no way and under no circumstances be controlled or modified, give this property to the murderer. [3] The purpose of those statutes was to enable testators to dispose of their estates to the objects of their county at death, and to carry into effect their final wishes legally expressed; and in considering and giving effect to them this purpose must be kept in view. [4] It was the intention of the law-makers that the donees in a will should have the property given to them. [5] But it never could have been their intention that a donee who murdered the testator to make the will operative should have any benefit under it. [6] If such a case had been present to their minds, and it had been supposed necessary to make some provision of law to meet it, it cannot be doubted that they would have provided for it. [7] It is a familiar canon of construction that a thing which is within the intention of the makers of a statute is as much within the statute as if it were within the letter; and a thing which is within the letter of the statute is not within the statute unless it be within the intention of the makers. [8] The writers of laws do not always express their intention perfectly, but either exceed it or fall short of it, so that judges are to collect it from probable or rational conjectures only, and this is called "rational interpretation"; [9] and Rutherford, in his Institutes (page 420), says: "Where we make use of rational interpretation, sometimes we restrain the meaning of the writer so as to take in less, and sometimes we extend or enlarge his meaning so as to take in more, than his words express." [10] Such a construction ought to be put upon a statute as will best answer the intention which the makers had in view, for *qui hoeret in litera, hoeret in cortice.* [11] In Bac. Abr. "Statute," 1, 5; Puff. Law Nat. bk. 5, c. 12; Ruth. Inst. 422, 427, and in Smith's Commentaries, 814, many cases are mentioned where it was held that matters embraced in the general words of statutes nevertheless were not within the statutes, because it could not have been the intention of the law-makers that they should be included. [12] They were taken out of the statutes by an equitable construction; [13] and it is said in Bacon: "By an equitable construction a case not within the letter of a statute is sometimes holden to be within the meaning, because it is within the mischief for which a remedy is provided. [14] The reason for such construction is that the law-makers could not set down every case in express terms. [15] In order to form a right judgment whether a case be within the equity of a statute, it is a good way to suppose the law-maker present, and that you have asked him this question: Did you intend to comprehend this case? **[16]** Then you must give yourself such answer as you imagine he, being an upright and reasonable man, would have given. If this be that he did mean to comprehend it, you may safely hold the case to be within the equity of the statute; for while you do no more than he would have done, you do not act contrary to the statute, but in conformity thereto." 9 Bac. Abr. 248. **[17]** In some cases the letter of a legislative act is restrained by an equitable construction; in others, it is enlarged; in others, the construction is contrary to the letter. . . . **[18]** If the law makers could, as to this case, be consulted, would they say that they intended by their general language that the property of a testator or of an ancestor should pass to one who had taken his life for the express purpose of getting his property? **[19]** In 1 Bl Comm. 91, the learned author, speaking of the construction of statutes, says: "If there arise out of them collaterally any absurd consequences manifestly contradictory to common reason, they are with regard to those collateral consequences void." . . . **[20]** There was a statute in Bologna that whoever drew blood in the streets should be severely punished, and yet it was held not to apply to the case of a barber who opened a vein in the street. **[21]** It is commanded in the decalogue that no work shall be done upon the Sabbath, and yet giving the command a rational interpretation founded upon its design the Infallible Judge held that it did not prohibit works of necessity, charity, or benevolence on that day.

{C}   **[1]** What could be more unreasonable than to suppose that it was the legislative intention in the general laws passed for the orderly, peaceable, and just devolution of property that they should have operation in favor of one who murdered his ancestor that he might speedily come into the possession of his estate? **[2]** Such an intention is inconceivable. **[3]** We need not, therefore, be much troubled by the general language contained in the laws. **[4]** Besides, all laws, as well as all contracts, may be controlled in their operation and effect by general, fundamental maxims of the common law. **[5]** No one shall be permitted to profit by his own fraud, or to take advantage of his own wrong, or to found any claim upon his own iniquity, or to acquire property by his own crime. **[6]** These maxims are dictated by public policy, have their foundation in universal law administered in all civilized countries, and have nowhere been superseded by statutes. **[7]** They were applied in the decision of the case of Insurance Co. v. Armstrong, 117 U. S. 599, 6 Sup. Ct. Rep. 877. **[8]** There it was held that the person who procured a policy upon the life of another, payable at his death, and then murdered the assured to make the policy payable, could not recover thereon. **[9]** Mr. Justice FIELD, writing the opinion, said: "Independently of any proof of the motives of Hunter in obtaining the policy, and even assuming that they were just and proper, he forfeited all rights under it when, to secure its immediate payment, he murdered the assured. **[10]** It would be a reproach to the jurisprudence of the country if one could recover insurance money payable on the death of a party whose life he had feloniously taken. **[11]** As well might he recover insurance money upon a building that he had willfully fired." **[12]** These maxims, without any statute giving them force or operation, frequently control the effect and nullify the language of wills. **[13]** A will procured by fraud and deception, like any other instrument, may be decreed void, and set aside; and so a particular portion of a will may be excluded from probate, or held inoperative, if induced by the fraud or undue influence of the person in whose favor it is. Allen v. McPherson, 1 H. L. Cas. 191; Harrison's Appeal, 48 Conn. 202. [14] So a will may contain provisions which are immoral, irreligious, or against public policy, and they will be held void.

{D}   [1] Here there was no certainty that this murderer would survive the testator, or that the testator would not change his will, and there was no certainty that he would get this property if nature was allowed to take its course. [2] He therefore murdered the testator expressly to vest himself with an estate. [3] Under such circumstances what law, human or divine, will allow him to take the estate and enjoy the fruits of his crime? [4] The will spoke and became operative at the death of the testator. [5] He caused that death, and thus by his crime made it speak and have operation. [6] Shall it speak and operate in his favor? [7] If he had met the testator, and taken his property by force, he would have had no title to it. [8] Shall he acquire title by murdering him? [9] If he had gone to the testator's house, and by force compelled him, or by fraud or undue influence had induced him, to will him his property, the law would not allow him to hold it. [10] But can he give effect and operation to a will by murder, and yet take the property? [11] To answer these questions in the affirmative it seems to me would be a reproach to the jurisprudence of our state, and an offense against public policy. [12] Under the civil law, evolved from the general principles of natural law and justice by many generations of jurisconsults, philosophers, and statesmen, one cannot take property by inheritance or will from an ancestor or benefactor whom he has murdered. Dom. Civil Law, pt. 2, bk. 1, tit. 1, § 3; Code Nap. § 727; Mack. Rom. Law, 530, 550. [13] In the Civil Code of Lower Canada the provisions on the subject in the Code Napoleon have been substantially copied. [14] But, so far as I can find, in no country where the common law prevails has it been deemed important to enact a law to provide for such a case. [15] Our revisers and law-makers were familiar with the civil law, and they did not deem it important to incorporate into our statutes its provisions upon this subject. [16] This is not a *casus omissus.* [17] It was evidently supposed that the maxims of the common law were sufficient to regulate such a case, and that a specific enactment for that purpose was not needed. [18] For the same reasons the defendant Palmer cannot take any of this property as heir. [19] Just before the murder he was not an heir, and it was not certain that he ever would be. [20] He might have died before his grandfather, or might have been disinherited by him. [21] He made himself an heir by the murder, and he seeks to take property as the fruit of his crime. [22] What has before been said to him as legatee applies to him with equal force as an heir. [23] He cannot vest himself with title by crime. [24] My view of this case does not inflict upon Elmer any greater or other punishment for his crime than the law specifies. [25] It takes from him no property, but simply holds that he shall not acquire property by his crime, and thus be rewarded for its commission.

{E}   [1] Our attention is called to Owens v. Owens, 100 N.C. 240, 6 S.E. Rep. 794, as a case quite like this. [2] There a wife had been convicted of being an accessory before the fact to the murder of her husband, and it was held that she was nevertheless entitled to dower. [3] I am unwilling to assent to the doctrine of that case. [4] The statutes provide dower for a wife who has the misfortune to survive her husband, and thus lose his support and protection. [5] It is clear beyond their purpose to make provision for a wife who by her own crime makes herself a widow, and willfully and intentionally deprives herself of the support and protection of her husband. [6] As she might have died before him, and thus never have been his widow, she cannot by her crime vest herself with an estate. [7] The principle which lies at the bottom of the maxim *volenti non fit injuria* should be applied to such a case, and a widow should not, for the purpose of acquiring, as such, property rights, be permitted to allege a widowhood which she has wickedly and intentionally created.

{F}   [1]The facts found entitled the plaintiffs to the relief they sought. [2] The error of the referee was in his conclusion of law. [3] Instead of granting a new trial, therefore, I think the proper judgment upon the facts found should be ordered here. [4] The facts have been passed upon twice with the same result—first upon the trial of Palmer for murder, and then by the referee in this action. [5] We are therefore of opinion that the ends of justice do not require that they should again come in question. [6] The judgment of the general term and that entered upon the report of the referee should therefore be reversed, and judgment should be entered as follows: That Elmer E. Palmer and the administrator be enjoined from using any of the personalty or real estate left by the testator for Elmer's benefit; that the devise and bequest in the will to Elmer be declared ineffective to pass the title to him; that by reason of the crime of murder committed upon the grandfather he is deprived of any interest in the estate left by him; that the plaintiffs are the true owners of the real and personal estate left by the testator, subject to the charge in favor of Elmer's mother and the widow of the testator, under the antenuptial agreement, and that the plaintiffs have costs in all the courts against Elmer. [7] All concur, except GRAY, J., who reads dissenting opinion, and DANFORTH, J., concurs.

GRAY, J. (dissenting)

{G}   [1] This appeal represents an extraordinary state of facts, and the case, in respect to them, I believe, is without precedent in this state. [2] The respondent, a lad of 16 years of age, being aware of the provisions in his grandfather's will, which constituted him the residuary legatee of the testator's estate, caused his death by poison, in 1882. [3] For this crime he was tried, and was convicted of murder in the second degree, and at the time of the commencement of this action he was serving out his sentence in the state reformatory. . . . [4] The question we are dealing with is whether a testamentary disposition can be altered, or a will revoked, after the testator's death, through an appeal to the courts, when the legislature has by its enactments prescribed exactly when and how wills may be made, altered, and revoked, and apparently, as it seems to me, when they have

been fully complied with, has left no room for the exercise of an equitable jurisdiction by courts over such matters. **[5]** Modern jurisprudence, in recognizing the
right of the individual, under more or less restrictions, to dispose of his property
after his death, subjects it to legislative control, both as to extent and as to mode
of exercise. **[6]** Complete freedom of testamentary disposition of one's property
has not been and is not the universal rule, as we see from the provisions of the
Napoleonic Code, from the systems of jurisprudence in countries which are mod-
eled upon the Roman law, and from the statutes of many of our states. **[7]** To the
statutory restraints which are imposed upon the disposition of one's property by
will are added strict and systematic statutory rules for the execution, alteration,
and revocation of the will, which must be, at least substantially, if not exactly, followed to insure validity and performance. **[8]** The reason for the establishment of
such rules, we may naturally assume, consists in the purpose to create those safeguards about these grave and important acts which experience has demonstrated
to be the wisest and surest. **[9]** That freedom which is permitted to be exercised
in the testamentary disposition of one's estate by the laws of the state is subject
to its being exercised in conformity with the regulations of the statutes. **[10]** The
capacity and the power of the individual to dispose of his property after death,
and the mode by which that power can be exercised, are matters of which the legislature has assumed the entire control, and has undertaken to regulate with comprehensive particularity.

{**H**}   **[1]** The appellants' argument is not helped by reference to those rules
of the civil law, or to those laws of other governments, by which the heir, or legatee, is excluded from benefit under the testament if he has been convicted of
killing, or attempting to kill, the testator. **[2]** In the absence of such legislation
here, the courts are not empowered to institute such a system of remedial justice.
[3] The deprivation of the heir of his testamentary succession by the Roman law,
when guilty of such a crime, plainly was intended to be in the nature of a punishment imposed upon him. The succession in such a case of guilt, escheated to the
exchequer. See Dom. Civil Law, pt. 2, bk. 1, tit. 1, § 3. **[4]** I concede that rules of
law which annul testamentary provisions made for the benefit of those who have
become unworthy of them may be based on principles of equity and of natural justice. **[5]** It is quite reasonable to suppose that a testator would revoke or alter his
will, where his mind has been so angered and changed as to make him unwilling
to have his will executed as it stood. **[6]** But these principles only suggest sufficient reasons for the enactment of laws to meet such cases.

{**I**}   **[1]** The statutes of this state have prescribed various ways in which a
will may be altered or revoked; but the very provision defining the modes of
alterations and revocation implies a prohibition of alteration or revocation in any
other way. **[2]** The words of the section of the statute are: "No will in writing,
except in the cases hereinafter mentioned, nor any part thereof, shall be revoked
or altered otherwise," etc. **[3]** Where, therefore, none of the cases mentioned
are met by the facts, and the revocation is not in the way described in the section, the will of the testator is unalterable. **[4]** I think that a valid will must continue as a will always, unless revoked in the manner provided by the statutes.

[5] Mere intention to revoke a will does not have the effect of revocation. [6] The intention to revoke is necessary to constitute the effective revocation of a will, but it must be demonstrated by one of the acts contemplated by the statute. [7] As WOODWORTH, J., said in Dan v. Brown, 4 Cow. 490: "Revocation is an act of the mind, which must be demonstrated by some outward and visible sign of relation." [8] The same learned judge said in that case: "The rule is that if the testator lets the will stand until he dies, it is his will; if he does not suffer it to do so, it is not his will." And see Goodright v. Glazier, 4 Burrows, 2512, 2514; Pemberton v. Pemberton, 13 Ves. 290. [9] The finding of fact of the referee that presumably the testator would have altered his will had he known of his grandson's murderous intent cannot affect the question. [10] We may concede it to the fullest extent; but still the cardinal objection is undisposed of—that the making and the revocation of a will are purely matters of statutory regulation, by which the court is bound in the determination of questions relating to these acts.

{J}   [1] Two cases—in this state and in Kentucky—at an early day, seem to me to be much in point. [2] Gains v. Gains, 2 A.K. Marsh 190, was decided by the Kentucky court of appeals in 1820. It was there urged that the testator intended to have destroyed his will, and that he was forcibly prevented from doing so by the defendant in error or devisee; and it was insisted that the will, though not expressly, was thereby virtually, revoked. [3] The court held, as the act concerning wills prescribed that manner in which a will might be revoked, that, as none of the acts evidencing revocation were done, the intention could not be substituted for the act. [4] In that case the will was snatched away, and forcibly retained. [5] In 1854, Surrogate BRADFORD, whose opinions are entitled to the highest consideration, decided the case of Leaycraft v. Simmons, 3 Bradf. Sur. 35. [6] In that case the testator, a man of 89 years of age, desired to make a codicil to his will, in order to enlarge the provisions for his daughter. [7] His son, having custody of the instrument, and the one to be prejudiced by the change, refused to produce the will at the testator's request, for the purpose of alteration. [8] The learned surrogate refers to the provisions of the civil law for such and other cases of unworthy conduct in the heir or legatee, and says: "Our statute has undertaken to prescribe the mode in which wills can be revoked eliciting the statutory provision. [9] This is the law by which I am governed in passing upon questions touching the revocation of wills. [10] The whole of this subject is now regulated by statute; and a mere intention to revoke, however well authenticated, or however defeated, is not sufficient." [11] And he held that the will must be admitted to probate. [12] I may refer also to a case in the Pennsylvania courts. [13] In that state the statute prescribed the mode for repealing or altering a will, and in Clingan v. Micheltree, 31 Pa. St. 25, the supreme court of the state held, where a will was kept from destruction by the fraud and misrepresentation of the devisee, that to declare it canceled as against the fraudulent party would be to enlarge the statute.

{K}   [1] I cannot find any support for the argument that the respondent's succession to the property should be avoided because of his criminal act, when the laws are silent. [2] Public policy does not demand it; for the demands of public policy are satisfied by the proper execution of the laws and the punishment of the crime. [3] There has been no convention between the testator and his legatee; nor is there any such contractual element, in such a disposition of property by a testator, as to impose or imply conditions in the legatee. [4] The appellants' argument practically amounts to this: that, as the legatee has been guilty of a crime, by the commission of which he is placed in a position to sooner receive the benefits of the testamentary provision, his rights to the property should be forfeited, and he should be divested of his estate. [5] To allow their argument to prevail would involve the diversion by the court of the testator's estate into the hands of persons whom, possibly enough, for all we know, the testator might not have chosen or desired as its recipients. [6] Practically the court is asked to make another will for the testator. [7] The laws do not warrant this judicial action, and mere presumption would not be strong enough to sustain it. [8] But, more than this, to concede the appellants' views would involve the imposition of an additional punishment or penalty upon the respondent. [9] What power or warrant have the courts to add to the respondent's penalties by depriving him of property? [10] The law has punished him for his crime, and we may not say that it was an insufficient punishment. [11] In the trial and punishment of the respondent the law has vindicated itself for the outrage which he committed, and further judicial utterance upon the subject of punishment or deprivation of rights is barred. [12] We may not, in the language of the court in People v. Thornton, 25 Hun. 456, "enhance the pains, penalties, and forfeitures provided by law for the punishment of crime." [13] The judgment should be affirmed, with costs.

DANFORTH, J., concurs.

5.2 Analysis of *Riggs v. Palmer*
Preliminaries

Facts   As stated by Justices Earl and Gray in their respective opinions [A1–4 and G2–3], the facts seem to be these: Francis Palmer executed a will in which he left a relatively small bequest to each of his two daughters, and left the remainder of his sizable estate to his grandson Elmer, who knew about the will's provisions. Some time later Francis apparently "manifested some intention" to modify his will and to revoke the provisions relating to Elmer's inheritance. Elmer learned of this, and before Francis could modify the will, Elmer poisoned him. Elmer was convicted of second-degree murder and sentenced to prison in a *criminal trial* [G3]. Note the following:

(1) *Riggs* is a *civil proceeding* (Appendix II.1.2.2) concerning only the disposition of the estate of Francis Palmer.

(2) Since Elmer is in prison, he might not be able to do much with his inheritance, but if the Court were to disqualify him as a beneficiary, then the large portion of the estate that Elmer was awarded would go back into the "estate pool," and would presumably then be available

to the other beneficiaries. (The "Riggs" mentioned in the title of this case is one of Francis Palmer's daughters, who are suing Elmer for the purpose of recovering his portion of the estate.)

Issue and Holding   Simply stated, the "narrow" question before the Court of Appeals of the State of New York is whether Elmer should inherit the property left to him in his grandfather's will, given that he murdered his grandfather in order to inherit. Readers who wish to be more careful about the statement of the issue, nonetheless, should review our discussion of it in section 4.2.2 and should notice that in the text of *Riggs* we find three distinct expressions of it: one in the summary, one from the author of the majority opinion [**A4**], and one from the author of the dissenting opinion [**G4**].

For a statement of the holding in *Riggs,* refer to the discussion in section 4.2.2.

Justice Earl's Majority Opinion

Judge Earl rules that Elmer *should not* inherit and supports his ruling with sustained, detailed argumentation. A quick reading of the text shows that the argumentative part of Judge Earl's opinion is expounded in paragraphs **B** through **E.** But where exactly do we start in order to unravel the arguments he offers?

We suggest that we begin at the beginning. For right at the start of Judge Earl's opinion we get a good clue as to the direction of his overall argument when we are confronted with Earl's explicit admission that Elmer *should* inherit *if* the statutes on wills are read literally and *if* the binding force and effect of wills cannot be broken. Given that Judge Earl's goal is to show that Elmer *should not* inherit, it seems reasonable to expect him to argue both against the literal interpretation of the statutes on wills as well as against a supposedly all-binding, never-alterable character of wills. Indeed, Judge Earl develops just this line of argument. A "bird's-eye view" of the text shows that Judge Earl's *overall argument* in support of his ruling, as expounded in paragraphs **B–E,** can be summarized as follows:

> The statutes on wills make Elmer an heir to his grandfather's property only if
> (a) these statutes are to be interpreted literally or (b) there can be no circumstances under which the force and binding effect of wills can be controlled and/or modified. However, (a) the statutes on wills need not be interpreted literally, and (b) even in the face of the literal terms of the statutes on wills, there can be circumstances under which the force and binding effect of wills can be controlled and/or modified. Thus the statutes on wills do not make Elmer an heir to his grandfather's property.

For simplicity and ease of reference, we can bring out explicitly the modus tollens form (section 2.4.2.1) of Judge Earl's main argument when we compress it even further as follows:

(1) *If* Elmer should inherit, *then* either the statutes on wills need to be interpreted literally or the binding force and effect of wills cannot be broken.

(2) *It is not the case that* either the statutes on wills need to be interpreted literally or the binding force and effect of wills cannot be broken.

---

(3) *It is not the case that* Elmer should inherit.

According to premise 1 of this argument, a *necessary condition* (section 1.3.2.3.2) for Elmer's inheriting the property is that the following *disjunction* (section 1.3.2.2)

(i) *Either* statutes on wills need to be interpreted literally *or* the binding force and effect of wills cannot be broken.

must be true. But disjunction (i), premise 2 says, is false. Thus, we can conclude by modus tollens that (premise 3) Elmer should not inherit.[1]

Clearly, the crucial premise, and the point in need of substantive and detailed argumentation, is premise 2. This premise is the negation of disjunction (i). We know that, in general, the negation of the disjunction "*X* or *Y*" can be expressed as "Neither *X* nor *Y*," which in turn is equivalent to "It is not the case that *X and* it is not the case that *Y*" (section 1.3.2.5). Thus to show that premise 2 of his main argument is true, Judge Earl needs to convincingly argue that both:

(ii) *It is not the case that* statutes on wills *need* be interpreted literally.

and

(iii) *It is not the case that* the binding force and effect of wills *cannot* be broken.

are true. Thus, in the remainder of his opinion, Judge Earl provides two subarguments designed to demonstrate the truth of (ii) and (iii) respectively. For convenience, we can label them and summarize the gist of them as follows:

(*I*) *The Argument against Literal Statutory Interpretation* [*B1–C3*]: The statutes on wills need not be construed literally but rather in light of the purposes and intentions of the legislators.

(II) *The Argument That Maxims Can Control Wills* [*C4–D25*]: As a matter of jurisprudence, wills are controlled by common law principles ("maxims") that are also part of the law.

---

[1]A note on the logic involved here: You may be confused that we present Earl's main argument as a modus tollens. To be sure, the way [**B2**] is expressed (that is, "statutes . . . *if* literally construed . . . *and if* their force and effect can in no way . . . be modified . . . give this property to the murderer") appears to give a *conjunction* (section 1.3.2.1) of two conditions as *sufficient* (section 1.3.2.3.2) for Elmer's inheriting. However, it is quite clear in the remainder of the argument that Judge Earl launches a systematic attack against each of these conditions. Thus, unless we wish to attribute to Earl some gross misunderstandings of logic, as, for example, arguing invalidly in a *denying the antecedent* fashion (section 2.4.2.2), we must assume that each "if" must be read as "only if" that is, as denoting a *necessary condition:* (sections 1.3.2.3.1 and 1.3.2.3.2), and the apparent *conjunction* must be understood as being meant as a *disjunction*.

Argument (I) purports to directly establish (ii), while argument (II) purports to establish (iii). Let us look at the details of each in turn.

(I) The Argument against Literal Statutory Interpretation

In **B1–C3,** Judge Earl argues directly for the truth of (ii). Unfortunately, Earl's argument here is not all that clearly laid out. In order to understand it, it may be best to start with the observation that Earl operates here under two distinct constraints. In the first place, *Riggs* is not a case where we have common law reliance on some prior *judicial* rule which Earl may have a (relatively) free hand to interpret. On the contrary, Earl is confronted with *statutes* on wills, statutes that are apparently free of *vagueness* or *ambiguity* (section 1.2.1), and which, under the *principle of separation of powers* (Appendix II.2.1) and the corollary *principle of legislative supremacy,* impose a considerable constraint on his freedom to rule as he pleases. In the second place, as it stands, the will of Francis Palmer is a valid will according to the statutes on wills; every formal feature of the will is in conformity with the statutes on wills "as literally construed" [**B1–2**]. So Judge Earl cannot point to anything within the will and argue that the will should be invalidated because of some shortcoming of the will itself (for example, not being signed, not properly witnessed, incomplete in some way).

Given that much, we should not be surprised that Earl begins his argument with the admission that the literal reading of the statutes on wills yields as a clear result that Elmer *should* have the property, the murder notwithstanding [**B2**]. Yet Judge Earl is out to make a case *against* Elmer's inheriting. Clearly, if he is to establish his case, he must argue that we can ignore the letter of the law. Indeed, this is exactly what he does in **B,** and he arrives at the conclusion, "We need not, therefore, be much troubled by the general language contained in the laws" [**C3**]. But how exactly does he establish this conclusion? Given the complexity of Earl's argument, it may be best to unfold it in "labeled" stages as follows:

*Step 1—There is (also) the purposive approach (which yields that Elmer should **not** inherit)* [**B1–6**]. Judge Earl starts by implicitly bringing to our attention the fact that the defendant's (Elmer's) case relies on the Court's adopting a literal interpretation of the statutes on wills (that is, adopting the *textualist approach*—section 3.4.1.1) [**B1**]. Immediately, however, Judge Earl makes us aware that the Court does not have to take the textualist approach. For there is an *alternative* to focusing on the text of the statutes, namely, the alternative of focusing on the *intention* or purpose of the legislature in enacting a statute (that is, the *purposive approach*—section 3.4.1.1—or "rational interpretation," as Earl calls it) [**B8**]. Adoption of this latter approach, moreover, yields that Elmer should *not* inherit, a result that *contradicts* (section 1.3.3) the one yielded by the literal interpretation of the statutes on wills. Why so? Because "it cannot be doubted," Earl asserts (but does not prove), that it could have never been the intention of the legislators to allow one who murders the testator in order to make the will operative to benefit from the will [**B3–6**].[2]

*Step 2—As a matter of jurisprudence, it is quite appropriate to pursue the purposive approach [**B7–17**].* So far, Judge Earl has established the rather weak point that there is an alternative to taking the literal approach (and that *if* the alternative is adopted, Elmer should not inherit). But what entitles us to the purposive approach anyway? That is, to what extent, if any, is it legitimate for the Court to seek legislative intent instead of merely focusing on the actual text of the statute?

The answer to this is found in **B7–B17**. There Judge Earl sets out to establish that a Court's taking the purposive approach to interpretation is a well-established practice in the legal community (and thus his opting for the purpose of the legislature in the statutes on wills is anything but a capricious move on his part). To this effect, he engages in an elaborate *argument from authority* (section 2.5.1) and cites numerous legal writers and treatises who both attest to the legitimacy of the "rational interpretation" in jurisprudence, while at the same time explicate its meaning, scope, and operation. All in all, we are told that seeking legislative intent is not only a legitimate legal avenue for the Court to take, but also one that, apparently, cannot be ignored in favor of exclusive focus on literal interpretation [**B7**].

*Step 3—In cases like the present one we must abandon literal statutory interpretation in favor of "rational interpretation" [**B19–C31**].* Up to this point, Judge Earl has established the propriety of a Court's usage of "rational interpretation." Thus he has established that the literal interpretation of the statutes on wills is not the only avenue available, because seeking legislative intent is also an *equally available and appropriate* avenue for the Court to take. To the degree that Judge Earl is interested in merely establishing that the Court *need not* pursue the literal interpretation of the statutes on wills, he has done enough. He has adequately proven claim (ii). Notice, however, that Judge Earl seems to take his case a step further, for he continues his argument by showing the much stronger point that in the present case, we *should not* adopt the literal interpretation. The argument here is rather complex, in part because of the fact that it is quite compressed. It seems to be as follows:

As we noted in section 3.4.1.1, when the literal interpretation of a statute yields absurd results, the literal understanding of the text is normally abandoned

---

[2]The brief subargument that Earl provides in **B3–6** seems to be this: The special intention of the legislature in passing the statutes on wills is to further the interests of testators by facilitating the orderly passing of their property according to their wishes [**B3**]. But there can be cases of *statutory indeterminacy due to gaps in the law* (section 3.4.1.1), since law makers are not omniscient and cannot anticipate all the possible cases that will arise under a statute. The case before us is one in which "it cannot be doubted" that it would have been handled differently had the legislators anticipated it.

Notice that *at this juncture* Earl finds, on intuitive grounds, that it is simply absurd to think that the legislators would have intentionally remained silent *in order to allow* a donee who murders the testator, for the purpose of making the will operative, to benefit from that will. As far as Earl sees it, at this point anyway, this special case simply has not been anticipated.

in favor of the spirit or purpose of the statute. In **B19–21,** Judge Earl seems to rely just on this when he argues both that legal authorities advise resorting to legislative intent when faced with absurdities resulting from a literal interpretation of a text, and that such recourse has, in fact, been taken in precedent cases. The rest of Judge Earl's argument here appears to rely on *analogical reasoning* (section 2.5.3.1) as follows: (a) in two precedent cases where literal interpretation of a statute led to absurd results, that interpretation was set aside [**B20–21**]; (b) the present case is similar to the precedent cases in that, if the statutes on wills are read literally, they too lead to an absurd result; (c) in the present case, the literal interpretation of the statute of wills *should* be set aside [**C3**].

Of course, the debatable premise is (b): just what exactly is the absurdity involved in reading the statutes on wills literally? Overall, Earl's subargument for this, compressed to the maximum as it may be, seems to take the form of a *hypothetical syllogism* (section 2.4.2.1) as follows: (1) If we read the statutes on wills literally, then we will be attributing to the legislators the special intention to allow possession of a property by those who murder a testator exactly in order to speedily possess that property. (2) If we attribute to the legislators the special intention to allow possession of a property by those who murder a testator exactly in order to speedily possess that property, we are led to an absurd result. (3) Thus, if we read the statutes on wills literally, then we are led to an absurd result.

Once more, the crucial premise of this last subargument is premise 2. Why is it true? The direct, albeit extremely compact, answer is given by Earl in **C1–C2** (but one needs to reread **B18** as well as **B3–6**). It can be reconstructed as follows: The *general intention* of the legislators of statutes on wills is to *benefit* testators by allowing them to determine in an "orderly and just way" what happens to their property after their death. But the (alleged) *special intention* of the legislators to allow possession of a property by those who murder a testator exactly in order to speedily possess that property cannot be for the benefit of the testator. (It is absurd to say that Elmer's killing his grandfather in order to speedily inherit from him was for the benefit of his grandfather.) Thus, if attributed to the legislators, the alleged special intention to allow murderers of testators to inherit from the testators contradicts the general intention of the same legislators to benefit testators[3]—and thus the absurdity, and the truth, of premise 2. And, going backward, thus is shown the truth of the debatable premise (b) stated earlier and, in turn, the truth of Earl's analogical reasoning to the stronger conclusion that the literal interpretation of the statutes on wills *should* be set aside in the present case. Justice Earl has now established claim (ii) of his main argument.

---

[3]Notice that the issue of intent arises in two contexts here: (i) the intent of the *legislators* in terms of creating statutes allowing people to dispose of their worldly goods, and (ii) the intent of the *testator* (Francis Palmer). Justice Earl seems to be arguing that the literal application of the statute would thwart the legislators' general intention regarding wills, as well as Francis Palmer's specific intention regarding Elmer.

(II) The Argument That Maxims Can Control Wills

Having established the truth of (ii), Judge Earl presses on with his main argument by arguing now directly for the truth of (iii), the claim that the force and binding effect of wills *can* be broken. His argument in support of (iii) begins at **C4** when, rather abruptly, he introduces a new element, namely, what he calls "maxims of common law." A bird's-eye view of the text shows that a series of sub-arguments revolve around this newly introduced notion, and that this line of arguing is sustained to the end of **D25.** Just like before, we can unfold the present argument in stages as follows.

Step 1—"Maxims of common law" are legitimate, albeit superior parts of the law[C4–C12]. Judge Earl starts his argument by claiming that there exist legitimate legal resources, namely, "general, fundamental maxims of the common law" that *may control* "all laws as well as all contracts" [**C4**]. This is a rather surprising and important view of the law. Just what exactly are these maxims, and where do they come from? When Judge Earl proceeds to give us such examples of maxims as "no one shall be permitted to profit by his own crime" [**C5**], we get the distinct impression that he has in mind general principles that embody a distinct *moral content.* These principles, we are told, do not have a statutory origin [**C12**] but are "dictated by public policy [and] have their foundation in universal law administered in all civilized countries" [**C6**].

Not only are maxims of common law part of the law, Judge Earl points out, they have a *prominent* position in the hierarchy of the law: they have "nowhere been superceded by statutes" [**C6**], but rather have the power to override and supersede statutes. In fact, maxims *have* controlled cases in the past. A case in point is *Insurance v. Armstrong,* a *contract* case (Appendix II.1.3.2) in which the court held without any statutory basis that a person who murdered the insured to make the benefits payable "forfeited all rights under the policy" and could not recover [**C7–11**].

Step 2—Maxims of common law can control wills [C12–14]: Having shown that maxims can control various areas of the law, Judge Earl brings the argument home by pointing out that maxims can also control *wills in particular.* Examples of how maxims override wills as literally written ("control the effect and nullify the language of wills"—[**C13**]) include the use of fraud, deception, and undue influence, as well as when wills are "immoral, irreligious or against public policy." So, when a will contains a provision, or is drawn up in such a way, that it conflicts with one of the maxims of common law, the maxim can override the will, rendering either the entire will or some of its provisions inoperative. All in all, Judge Earl seems to say, a will's violating the common law maxims is a *sufficient condition* (section 1.3.2.3.2) for breaking the effect and binding force of that will (that is, for the will to be held inoperative). All that Judge Earl needs now in order to complete this argument is to point out that the present case of murdering the testator in order to inherit from him is just another occasion of violating common law maxims, an occasion that suffices to render an otherwise valid will inoperative. This is the task undertaken in the third and final step of this argument.

Step 3—Maxims of common law should also control the present will (to the effect that Elmer should not inherit) [D1–25]. The final step of Judge Earl's argument begins by reminding us that Elmer is not an heir *simpliciter,* but rather *an heir by virtue of having murdered the testator specifically in order to inherit from him* (call him for brevity "heir-by-murder") [**D1–5**]. The crucial question for Judge Earl is whether an heir-by-murder is a *legally proper* heir entitled to the property [**D10**]. An affirmative answer to this, Judge Earl claims, "would be a reproach to the jurisprudence of this state, and an offence against public policy" [**D11**], and he proceeds to justify his claim with two distinct subarguments as follows:

1. *The Analogical Argument [D7–11]:* An heir-by-murder is one who acquires property as the fruit of his own crime. But in relevantly similar hypothetical cases where property is acquired by criminal force or fraud, the law would not allow title to the property thus acquired. Therefore, by *analogical reasoning* (section 2.3.5), if the Court were to treat *Riggs* in a relevantly similar manner, it must disallow Elmer's claim on the estate.

2. *The Overriding Authority of Principles Argument [D12–25]:* In systems of law that evolved from principles of *natural law* (Appendix II.1) and that are dominated by written codes, we find *statutory regulation* to the effect that one cannot be the heir of one whom he has murdered. But in a system of common law like ours, the absence of such statutory regulation is not an oversight. There is *no need for the legislature* to issue a mandate making "murder of the testator by the beneficiary" one of the invalidating conditions of wills, since such a mandate is *already contained in the maxims* of common law.[4] In view of the prominent legal status of these maxims in our system (step 1), and in view of the fact that the violation of these maxims is a sufficient condition for holding a will inoperative (step 2), the Court must override the literal terms of Francis's will and find that Elmer is not a *proper* heir ("He cannot vest himself with title by crime" [**D23**]). Once again, the Court must recognize that the force and binding effect of Francis's will must be broken and thus disallow Elmer's claim on the estate.

Taken together, the "overriding authority of principles argument" and the "analogical argument" given in step 3 of Judge Earl's argument establish his point that, in view of his crime, Elmer is a proper heir to his grandfather's property *only on pain of violating the maxims of common law.* Yet given the legal

---

[4]This point involves, again, an appeal to the actions and intentions of the legislators, but here the appeal is slightly different. Here Justice Earl attributes to them a specific view of the law (that it includes maxims), and makes an inference about their intentions and actions based on their holding that view of the law (they would have seen a statute addressing the facts in *Riggs* as being *unnecessary*). Notice that this differs from what he says in **B3-6** where he seems to argue that *Riggs* was *unanticipated* by the legislators (see note 2).

status and the overriding power of these maxims (established in steps 1 and 2), the Court must recognize that the force and binding effect of Francis's will *must* be broken. Therefore, claim (iii) is true.

Concluding Remarks on Judge Earl's Opinion

Having argued for the truth of both claims (ii) and (iii), Judge Earl should be now ready to proceed and issue his decision to disinherit Elmer. Yet, there is still an issue that he needs to address before he proceeds, namely, the issue of whether his view in this case puts him at odds with *stare decisis* (section 3.3.3). He tangles with this issue in **E1–7**.

Notice that in the process of his argument, Judge Earl has given an interesting twist to the case. All along, the defense (Elmer's side) seems to have relied on the assumption that the validity of the grandfather's will is a legally *sufficient* condition for Elmer to inherit. Judge Earl, however, turns the tables when, in effect, he shows that the validity of a will is merely a *necessary* condition for Elmer to inherit. What is worse for the defense, moreover, is that Judge Earl's *argument that maxims can control wills* shows that a *sufficient* condition for holding inoperative an otherwise valid will is that its operation would violate the dictates of common law maxims. But here is the crucial point: is violation of common law maxims indeed sufficient for invalidating a will?

Precedent seems to show that violation of common law maxims is *not* sufficient for invalidating a will. The case in point is *Owens v. Owens* in which a wife murdered her husband, but nonetheless was allowed to inherit [**E1–2**]. *Owens* appears to be a clear counterexample to Judge Earl's position, since undoubtedly it is in violation of the common law maxim "no one should profit from his own wrongdoing." Given that much, one might expect Justice Earl to attempt to *distinguish precedent* (section 3.3.3) by producing a set of significant relevant dissimilarities between *Riggs* and *Owens* that justify him in *refuting the analogy* (section 2.5.3.3) between these two cases. Interestingly enough, he does no such thing. On the contrary, he turns the case on its head and uses it to *reinforce his own position:* he announces that he is "unwilling to assent to the doctrine of that case" [**E3**] and argues that, since *Owens* is very much *like Riggs* (principles of common law have been violated in both cases), it should have been decided differently [**E4–7**]. Presumably, Judge Earl is quite confident in his own line of reasoning.

Justice Gray's Dissent

Justice Gray counters the majority opinion with four independent arguments of his own, designed to establish that, as a matter of law and regardless of our feelings in this case, Elmer Palmer should retain title to his share of the estate as stipulated by his grandfather's will. The exposition of Judge Gray's arguments in **G–K** is more or less straightforward. For simplicity, we label the arguments in a manner that captures their gist.

Argument 1—Statutory regulation of wills ought to reign supreme [G4–10]. The first argument that Judge Gray provides is a *direct* one in support of his view that the Court should not go against the letter of the law of the statutes on wills and revoke Francis's will. It occurs in **G4–10** and can be summarized in a *modus ponens* fashion (section 2.4.2.1) as follows:

(1) If the legislature has enacted direct and detailed statutes controlling matters on wills, the courts should not undertake the task of regulating those matters.

(2) The legislature has enacted direct and detailed statutes controlling matters on wills.

Thus,

(3) the courts should not undertake the task of regulating those matters.

The first premise of this argument is nowhere explicitly brought out; nor is its truth argued for by Judge Gray. Presumably, this is because its truth is unquestionable in any system of law that, like our own, abides by the *doctrine of separation of powers* (section 3.2.1) and the corollary *principle of legislative supremacy* (section 4.2). Thus the bulk of Judge Gray's argument is directed in substantiating premise (2). To this effect, Judge Gray painfully reminds anyone who is inclined to forget the legislature's role in this case that, both in our system of law as well as in others, the legislature has taken upon itself to provide *excessive* and *detailed* regulation of *all* matters pertaining to wills [**G6–9**]. Indeed, Gray tells us, matters of wills are matters for which "the legislature has assumed the entire control" [**G10**]. It follows that, however inequitable it may seem to allow Elmer to inherit in the circumstances, the Court has no choice but to abide by the statutes (and thus award the property to Elmer).

*Argument 2—Appeal to principles of common law is not sufficient to revoke a will [**H1–6**].* In the course of his *argument that maxims can control wills,* Judge Earl contended that the violation of common law principles is a *sufficient condition* for revoking an otherwise valid will. In the second argument for his dissent, Judge Gray *indirectly* supports his own position (that is, that Elmer should inherit) when he challenges his opponent's (Judge Earl's) contention. He does that when he briefly argues that the presumed *institutional authority* (section 2.5.1.2) of common law principles in *our* legal system can be *denied* on account of the *doctrine of separation of powers* (Appendix II.2.1) and the corollary *principle of legislative supremacy* as follows: Rules of law of foreign legal systems based on "common law maxims" were instituted in *those* systems with an eye to providing a system of remedial justice [**H2–3**]. But in *our* legal system, these laws have no legally binding authority. For the *doctrine of separation of powers* contained in *our* system does not allow the courts "to institute such a system of remedial justice" in cases where the rules enacted by the legislators seem to produce inequitable results. On the contrary, this doctrine obliges the Court to merely apply the rules that are enacted by the legislators. If, as *Riggs* points out, there is a defect in the rules, this can only be a reason for the Court to call for the legislators to "return to the drawing board" and revise the rules so as to remedy this defect [**H6**].

Argument 3—The intention to revoke a will is not sufficient for revoking a will [I1–J13]. A bird's-eye view of paragraphs I–J suggests that Judge Gray's next main concern is the issue of whether a testator's intention to revoke the will is a sufficient condition for a Court's allowing that will's revocation. Why such a concern? Presumably, Judge Gray's strategy here is to *indirectly* strengthen his own position (that is, to allow the will to stand) by challenging those who oppose it with an argument like the following:

(1) A testator's intention to revoke a will that was in fact left unaltered at the time of the testator's death is a sufficient condition for the Court's revoking that will.

(2) In *Riggs* we have the testator's intention to revoke his will.

(3) The Court should revoke the *Riggs* will.

Though, apparently, this argument has not been in fact provided by his opponents, Judge Gray anticipates its force: it captures a commonsense intuition that, as a matter of fairness, the Court should revoke Francis's will, since this is what Francis himself would have done had he had the chance to act. Indeed, according to Judge Earl's statement of the facts, Francis had in fact expressed an intention to revoke his will [A3]. And even if he had not, to Judge Gray's admission, we may reasonably suppose that he would have, had he learned of his grandson's intention to murder him [H5].

When Judge Gray sets out to challenge the preceding argument, he focuses on premise (1). Should intention to revoke a will be a sufficient condition for the Court to revoke it, as (1) has it? Judge Gray believes that the answer to this ought to be negative ("mere intention to revoke does not have the effect of revocation" [I5]), and he justifies his answer by means of three distinct subarguments:

- *Subargument 3a—Wills can only be revoked in the manner provided by the state's statutes [I1–4].* The first subargument provided against premise (1) directs us to the actual text of the statutes on wills. The text of the law, Judge Gray tells us, is perfectly clear and exact: a will can be revoked when and only when there is an occasion explicitly specified in the statute [I2]. Since the revocation of a will on account of the testator's intention to revoke is not listed among those occasions enumerated in the statute, such revocation is not warranted.

- *Subargument 3b—Legal authority supports the view that intention to revoke is not sufficient for revocation [I6–10].* Though intention to revoke a will is a *necessary* condition for a will's revocation, it is not a *sufficient* condition. Judge Gray's argument for this is a straightforward *reasoning from authority* (section 2.5.1). Legal authority, Judge Gray tells us, supports his view that since Francis Palmer's will was not in fact altered, whatever his intentions might have been, his will "is unalterable."

- *Subargument 3c—Precedent supports the view that intention to revoke is not sufficient for revocation [J1–13].* The final subargument involves a straightforward application of *analogical reasoning* (section 2.5.3). There are three cases from *precedent* (section 3.3.3), Justice Gray tells us, that clearly support his position that intention to revoke the will in *Riggs* is not a sufficient condition for its revocation. In each of these precedent cases, the court held that the bequest must stand as stipulated by the will according to statute, even though there was good reason to think that the testator would have altered the will if given the chance, and even though the actions of the beneficiary were criminal and reprehensible. Given the relevant similarity of these cases to *Riggs,* by analogical reasoning we must conclude that the Court must let Elmer's award stand.

Argument 4—Additional reasons not to disinherit Elmer [K1–13]. In his last argument, Judge Gray attacks what we may call the "summary position" of his opponents, namely, the position that, in view of Elmer's crime, and in view of the absence of statutory regulation of disinheriting an "heir-by-crime," it should be up to the Court to disinherit him [**K1 and K**4]. Judge Gray's challenge to this position is twofold. First, it should be noted, he tells us, that the Court does not *have* to take such stance, since that would not be demanded by public policy [**K2**]. Moreover, the following two reasons, he cautions us, speak against allowing the Court to revoke Francis Palmer's will:

- *Reason 1—Courts should not rewrite wills [K5–7].* If the Court invalidates Elmer's claim, it would be, in effect, making a new will for Francis, since it would then allow the property to pass on to Francis's two daughters. The question is: What grounds do we have for concluding that *this* is what Francis would have done with the property had he disinherited Elmer? The answer, of course, is that we have little if any ground for this claim. For all we know, Francis might not have cared much for his two daughters either, and might have awarded Elmer's share to anyone but them (after all, he did not leave his estate to them initially). We simply do not know what Francis would have done if given the chance to modify his will, and the Court is, in effect, rewriting his will for him without any guidance to speak of.
- *Reason 2—Courts should not engage in "double jeopardy" [K8–13].* We should not forget that Elmer has already been punished for his crime of murdering his grandfather: he was tried and convicted of second-degree murder in the criminal courts. But given that the criminal court has already decided Elmer's appropriate punishment for murdering his grandfather, for this Court to disinherit Elmer *on grounds that he is an "heir-by-crime"* would be, in effect, to punish him *twice* for the same crime. Yet, neither this Court nor any other Court should have the power to punish anyone more than once for the same deed.

For these reasons, Justice Gray concludes, the Court must reaffirm Elmer's inheritance as stipulated by his grandfather's will.

TO THINK ABOUT

(1) This case figures prominently in the development of noted legal scholar Ronald Dworkin's views on the nature of law, in particular his idea that judges appeal to legal principles (as opposed to legal rules) in deciding hard cases. To what extent do you think the resort to principle ("maxims of common law") determined this case?

(2) Principles of law ("common law maxims"), according to Ronald Dworkin, embody a distinct moral content. Do the principles cited by Judge Earl in **C5** fulfill the bill? What do you think is the exact role of morality in this case? How does it differ, if at all, from the dictates of public policy? Should morality dictate legal results?

(3) Justices Earl and Gray provide different statements of the facts and the issue in controversy. Are these statements indicative of their opposing attitudes and arguments in the case? Does Gray's statement of the facts in **G4,** for example, seem to demonstrate his determination to stick with the letter of the law?

(4) In *Riggs,* Judges Earl and Gray take conflicting approaches on the issue of statutory interpretation. Who do you think is right? What are the reasons for preferring one approach rather than the other?

(5) Suppose that in some future day after *Riggs,* a grandson who, like in *Riggs,* knows that he is the beneficiary of his grandfather's will, accidentally kills his grandfather. In deciding whether the grandson should inherit, should the Court in this case focus on the statutes on wills or on the *Riggs* precedent? What do you think is the role of *mens rea* (Appendix II.1.4) in deciding the similarities and differences between *Riggs* and this case?

5.3 *PALSGRAF V. LONG ISLAND RAILROAD*

PALSGRAF V. THE LONG ISLAND RAILROAD CO.
Court of Appeals of New York
248 N.Y. 339; 162 N.E. 99 (1928)

CARDOZO, CH. J.

{A}   [1] Plaintiff was standing on a platform of defendant's railroad after buying a ticket to go to Rockaway Beach. [2] A train stopped at the station, bound for another place. [3] Two men ran forward to catch it. [4] One of the men reached the platform of the car without mishap, though the train was already moving. [5] The other man, carrying a package, jumped aboard the car, but seemed unsteady as if about to fall. [6] A guard on the car, who had held the door open, reached forward to help him in, and another guard on the platform pushed him from behind. In this act, the package was dislodged, and fell upon the rails. [7] It was a package of small size, about fifteen inches long, and was covered by a newspaper. [8] In fact it contained fireworks, but there was nothing in its appearance to give notice of its contents. [9] The fireworks when they fell exploded. [10] The shock of the explosion threw down some scales at the other end of the platform, many feet away. [11] The scales struck the plaintiff, causing injuries for which she sues.

{B}   [1] The conduct of the defendant's guard, if a wrong in its relation to the holder of the package, was not a wrong in its relation to the plaintiff, standing far away. [2] Relatively to her it was not negligence at all. [3] Nothing in the situation gave notice that the falling package had in it the potency of peril to persons thus removed. [4] Negligence is not actionable unless it involves in the invasion of a legally protected interest, the violation of a right. [5] "Proof of negligence in the air, so to speak, will not do" (Pollock, Torts [11th ed.], p. 455). . . . [6] The plaintiff as she stood upon the platform of the station might claim to be protected against intentional invasion of her bodily security. [7] Such invasion is not charged. [8] She might claim to be protected against unintentional invasion by conduct involving in the thought of reasonable men an unreasonable hazard that such invasion would ensue. [9] These, from the point of view of the law, were the bounds of her immunity, with perhaps some rare exceptions, survivals for the most part of ancient forms of liability, where conduct is held to be at the peril of the actor (Sullivan v. Dunham, 161 N.Y. 290). [10] If no hazard was apparent to the eye of ordinary vigilance, an act innocent and harmless, at least to outward seeming, with reference to her, did not take to itself the quality of a tort because it happened to be a wrong, though apparently not one involving the risk of bodily insecurity, with reference to someone else. [11] "In every instance, before negligence can be predicated of a given act, back of the act must be sought and found a duty to the individual complaining, the observance of which would have averted or the injury" (W. Va. Central R. Co. v. State, 96 Md. 652, 666). . . . [12] "The ideas of negligence and duty are strictly correlative" (Thomas v. Quartermaine, 18 Q.B.D. 685, 694). [13] The plaintiff sues in her own right for a wrong personal to her, and not as the vicarious beneficiary of a breach of duty to another. . . .

{C}   [1] In this case, the rights that are said to have been violated, the interests said to have been invaded, are not even of the same order. [2] The man was not injured in his person nor even put in danger. [3] The purpose of the act, as well as its effect, was to make his person safe. [4] If there was a wrong to him at all, which may very well be doubted, it was a wrong to a property interest only, the safety of his package. [5] Out of this wrong to property, which threatened injury to nothing else, there has passed, we are told, to the plaintiff by derivation or succession a right of action for the invasion of an interest of another order, the right to bodily security. [6] The diversity of interests emphasizes the futility of the effort to build the plaintiff's right upon the basis of a wrong to some one else. [7] The gain is one of emphasis, for a like result would follow if the interests were the same. [8] Even then, the orbit of the danger as disclosed to the eye of reasonable vigilance would be the orbit of the duty. [9] One who jostles one's neighbor in a crowd does not invade the rights of others standing at the outer fringe when the unintended contact casts a bomb upon the ground. [10] The wrongdoer, as to them is the man who carries the bomb, not the one who explodes it without suspicion of the danger. [11] Life will have to be made over, and human nature transformed, before prevision so extravagant can be accepted as the norm of conduct, the customary standard to which behavior must conform.

{D}   [1] The argument for the plaintiff is built upon the shifting meanings of such words as "wrong" and "wrongful," and shares their instability. [2] What the plaintiff must show is "a wrong" to herself, i.e., a violation of her own right, and not merely a wrong to some one else, nor conduct "wrongful" because unsocial, but not "a wrong" to any one. [3] We are told that one who drives at reckless speed through a crowded city street is guilty of a negligent act and, therefore, of a wrongful one irrespective of the consequences. [4] Negligent the act is, and wrongful in the sense that it is unsocial, but wrongful and unsocial in relation to other travelers, only because the eye of vigilance perceives the risk of damage. [5] If the same act were to be committed on a speedway or a race course, it would lose its wrongful quality. [6] The risk reasonably to be perceived defines the duty to be obeyed, and risk imports relation; it is risk to another or to others within the range of apprehension. . . . [7] The range of reasonable apprehension is at times a question for the court, and at times, if varying inferences are possible, a question for the jury. [8] Here, by concession, there was nothing in the situation to suggest to the most cautious mind that the parcel wrapped in newspaper would spread wreckage through the station. [9] If the guard had thrown it down knowingly and willfully, he would not have threatened the plaintiff's safety, so far as appearances could warn him. [10] His conduct would not have involved, even then, an unreasonable probability of invasion of her bodily security. [11] Liability can be no greater where the act is inadvertent.

{E}   [1] Negligence, like risk, is thus a term of relation. [2] Negligence in the abstract, apart from things related, is surely not a tort, if indeed it is understandable at all. . . [3] Negligence is not a tort unless it results in the commission of a wrong, and the commission of a wrong imports the violation of a right, in this case, we are told, the right to be protected against interference with one's bodily security. [4] But bodily security is protected, not against all forms of interference or aggression, but only against some. [5] One who seeks redress at law does not make out a cause of action by showing without more that there has been damage to his person. [6] If the harm was not willful, he must show that the act as to him had possibilities of danger so many and apparent as to entitle him to be protected against the doing of it though the harm was unintended. [7] Affront to personality is still the keynote of the wrong. . . .

{F}   [1] The law of causation, remote or proximate, is thus foreign to the case before us. [2] The question of liability is always anterior to the question of the measure of the consequences that go with liability. [3] If there is no tort to be redressed, there is no occasion to consider what damage might be recovered if there were a finding of a tort. . . .

{G}   [1] The judgment of the Appellate Division and that of the Trial Term should be reversed, and the complaint dismissed, with costs in all courts.

ANDREWS, J. (dissenting)

{H}   [1] Assisting a passenger to board a train, the defendant's servant negligently knocked a package from his arms. It fell between the platform and the cars. [2] Of its contents the servant knew and could know nothing. [3] A violent explosion followed. [4] The concussion broke some scales standing a considerable distance away. In falling they injured the plaintiff, an intending passenger.

{I}   [1] Upon these facts may she recover the damages she has suffered in an action brought against the master? [2] The result we shall reach depends upon our theory as to the nature of negligence. [3] Is it a relative concept—the breach of some duty owing to a particular person or to particular persons? [4] Or where there is an act which unreasonably threatens the safety of others, is the doer liable for all its proximate consequences, even where they result in injury to one who would generally be thought to be outside the radius of danger? [5] This is not a mere dispute as to words. [6] We might not believe that to the average mind the dropping of the bundle would seem to involve the probability of harm to the plaintiff standing many feet away whatever might be the case as to the owner or to one so near as to be likely to be struck by its fall. [7] If, however, we adopt the second hypothesis we have to inquire only as to the relation between cause and effect. [8] We deal in terms of proximate cause, not of negligence. . . .

{J}   [1] But we are told that "there is no negligence unless there is in the particular case a legal duty to take care, and this duty must be one which is owed to the plaintiff himself and not merely to others" (Salmond, Torts [6th ed.], 24.). [2] This, I think, is too narrow a conception. [3] Where there is the unreasonable act, and some right that may be affected there is negligence whether damage does or does not result. [4] That is immaterial. [5] Should we drive down Broadway at a reckless speed, we are negligent whether we strike an approaching car or miss it by an inch. [6] The act itself is wrongful. [7] It is a wrong not only to those who happen to be within the radius of danger but to all who might have been there—a wrong to the public at large. [8] Such is the language of the street. [9] Such is the language of the courts when speaking of contributory negligence. . . . [10] Due care is a duty imposed on each one of us to protect society from unnecessary danger, not to protect A, B or C alone.

{K}   [1] It may well be that there is no such thing as negligence in the abstract. [2] "Proof of negligence in the air, so to speak, will not do." [3] In an empty world negligence would not exist. [4] It does involve a relationship between man and his fellows. [5] But not merely a relationship between man and those whom he might reasonably expect his act would injure. [6] Rather, a relationship between him and those whom he does in fact injure. [7] If his act has a tendency to harm some one, it harms him a mile away as surely as it does those on the scene. . . .

{L}   [1] The proposition is this. [2] Every one owes to the world at large the duty of refraining from those acts that may unreasonably threaten the safety of others. [3] Such an act occurs. [4] Not only is he wronged to whom harm might reasonably be expected to result, but he also who is in fact injured, even if he be outside what would generally be thought the danger zone. [5] There needs be duty due the one complaining but this is not a duty to a particular individual because as to him harm might be expected. [6] Harm to some one being the natural result of the act, not only that one alone, but all those in fact injured may complain. [7] We have never, I think, held otherwise. [8] Indeed in the *Di Caprio* case we said that a breach of a general ordinance defining the degree of care to be exercised in one's calling is evidence of negligence as to every one. [9] We did not limit this statement to those who might be expected to be exposed to danger. [10] Unreasonable risk being taken, its consequences are not confined to those who might probably be hurt.

{M}   [1] If this be so, we do not have a plaintiff suing by "derivation or succession." [2] Her action is original and primary. [3] Her claim is for a breach of duty to herself—not that she is subrogated to any right of action of the owner of the parcel or of a passenger standing at the scene of the explosion.

{N}   [1] The right to recover damages rests on additional considerations. [2] The plaintiff's rights must be injured, and this injury must be caused by the negligence. [3] We build a dam, but are negligent as to its foundations. [4] Breaking, it injures property down stream. [5] We are not liable if all this happened because of some reason other than the insecure foundation. [6] But when injuries do result from our unlawful act we are liable for the consequences. [7] It does not matter that they are unusual, unexpected, unforeseen and unforeseeable. [8] But there is one limitation. [9] The damages must be so connected with the negligence that the latter may be said to be the proximate cause of the former.

{O}   [1] These two words have never been given an inclusive definition. [2] What is a cause in a legal sense, still more what is a proximate cause, depend in each case upon many considerations, as does the existence of negligence itself. [3] Any philosophical doctrine of causation does not help us. . . . [4] A boy throws a stone into a pond. [5] The ripples spread. [6] The water level rises. [7] The history of that pond is altered to all eternity. [8] It will be altered by other causes also. [9] Yet it will be forever the resultant of all causes combined. [10] Each one will have an influence. [11] How great only omniscience can say. [12] You may speak of a chain, or if you please, a net. [13] An analogy is of little aid. [14] Each cause brings about future events. [15] Without each the future would not be the same. [16] Each is proximate in the sense it is essential. [17] But that is not what we mean by the word. . . . [18] What we do mean by the word "approximate" is, that because of convenience, of public policy, of a rough sense of justice, the law arbitrarily declines to trace a series of events beyond a certain point. [19] This is not logic, it is practical politics. [20] Take our rule as to fires. [21] Sparks from my burning haystack set on fire my house and my neighbor's. [22] I may recover from a negligent railroad. [23] He may not. [24] Yet the wrongful act as directly harmed the one as the other. [25] We may regret that the line was drawn just where it was, but drawn somewhere it had to be. . . .

{P}   [1] Take the illustration given in an unpublished manuscript by a distinguished and helpful writer on the law of torts. [2] A chauffeur negligently collides with another car which is filled with dynamite, although he could not know it. [3] An explosion follows. [4] A, walking on the sidewalk nearby, is killed. [5] B, sitting in a window of a building opposite, is cut by flying glass. [6] C, likewise sitting in a window a block away, is similarly injured. [7] And a further illustration. [8] A nursemaid, ten blocks away, startled by the noise, involuntarily drops a baby from her arms to the walk. [9] We are told that C may not recover while A may. [10] As to B it is a question for court or jury. [11] We will all agree that the baby might not. [12] Because, we are again told, the chauffeur had no reason to believe his conduct involved any risk of injuring either C or the baby. [13] As to them he was not negligent.

{Q}   [1] But the chauffeur, being negligent in risking the collision, his belief that the scope of the harm he might do would be limited is immaterial. [2] His act unreasonably jeopardized the safety of any one who might be affected by it. [3] C's injury and that of the baby were directly traceable to the collision. [4] Without that, the injury would not have happened. [5] C had the right to sit in his office, secure from such dangers. [6] The baby was entitled to use the sidewalk with reasonable safety.

{R}   [1] The true theory is, it seems to me, that the injury to C, if in truth he is to be denied recovery, and the injury to the baby is that their several injuries were not the proximate result of the negligence. [2] And here not what the chauffeur had reason to believe would be the result of his conduct, but what the prudent would foresee, may have a bearing. [3] May have some bearing, for the problem of proximate cause is not to be solved by any one consideration.

{S}   [1] It is all a question of expediency. [2] There are no fixed rules to govern our judgment. [3] There are simply matters of which we may take account. . . . [4] There are some hints that may help us. [5] The proximate cause, involved as it may be with many other causes, must be, at the least, something without which the event would not happen. [6] The court must ask itself whether there was a natural and continuous sequence between cause and effect. [7] Was the one a substantial factor in producing the other? [8] Was there a direct connection between them, without too many intervening causes? [9] Is the effect of cause on result not too attenuated? [10] Is the cause likely, in the usual judgment of mankind, to produce the result? [11] Or by the exercise of prudent foresight could the result be foreseen? [12] Is the result too remote from the cause, and here we consider remoteness in time and space? . . . [13] Clearly we must so consider, for the greater the distance either in time or space, the more surely do other causes intervene to affect the result. [14] When a lantern is overturned the firing of a shed is a fairly direct consequence. [15] Many things contribute to the spread of the conflagration—the force of the wind, the direction and width of street, the character of intervening structures, other factors. [16] We draw an uncertain and wavering line, but draw it we must as best we can.

{T}   [1] Once again, it is all a question of fair judgment, always keeping in mind the fact that we endeavor to make a rule in each case that will be practical and in keeping with the general understanding of mankind.

{U}   [1] Here another question must be answered. [2] In the case supposed it is said, and said correctly, that the chauffeur is liable for the direct effect of the explosion although he had no reason to suppose it would follow a collision. [3] The fact that the injury occurred in a different manner than that which might have been expected does not prevent the chauffeur's negligence from being in law the cause of the injury. [4] But the natural results of a negligent act—the results which a prudent man would or should foresee—do have a bearing upon the decision as to proximate cause. [5] We have said so repeatedly. [6] What should be foreseen? [7] No human foresight would suggest that a collision itself might injure one a block away. [8] On the contrary, given an explosion, such a possibility might be reasonably expected. [9] I think the direct connection, the foresight of which the courts speak, assumes prevision of the explosion, for the immediate results of which, at least, the chauffeur is responsible.

{V}   [1] It may be said this is unjust. [2] Why? [3] In fairness he should make good every injury flowing from his negligence. [4] Not because of tenderness toward him we say he need not answer for all that follows his wrong. [5] We look back to the catastrophe, the fire kindled by the spark, or the explosion. [6] We trace the consequences—not indefinitely, but to a certain point. [7] And to aid us in fixing that point we ask what might ordinarily be expected to follow the fire or the explosion.

{W}   [1] This last suggestion is the factor which must determine the case before us. [2] The act upon which defendant's liability rests is knocking an apparently harmless package onto the platform. [3] The act was negligent. [4] For its proximate consequences the defendant is liable. [5] If its contents were broken, to the owner; if it fell upon and crushed a passenger's foot, then to him. [6] If it exploded and injured one in the immediate vicinity, to him also as to A in the illustration. [7] Mrs. Palsgraf was standing some distance away. [8] How far cannot be told from the record—apparently twenty-five or thirty feet. [9] Perhaps less. [10] Except for the explosion, she would not have been injured. [11] We are told by the appellant in his brief "it cannot be denied that the explosion was the direct cause of the plaintiff's injuries." [12] So it was a substantial factor in producing the result—there was here a natural and continuous sequence—direct connection. [13] The only intervening cause was that instead of blowing her to the ground the concussion smashed the weighing machine which in turn fell upon her. [14] There was no remoteness in time, little in space. [15] And surely, given such an explosion as here it needed no great foresight to predict that the natural result would be to injure one on the platform at no greater distance from its scene than was the plaintiff. [16] Just how no one might be able to predict. [17] Whether by flying fragments, by broken glass, by wreckage of machines or structures no one could say. [18] But injury in some form was most probable.

{X}   [1] Under these circumstances I cannot say as a matter of law that the plaintiff's injuries were not the proximate result of the negligence. [2] That is all we have before us. [3] The court refused to so charge. [4] No request was made to submit the matter to the jury as a question of fact, even would that have been proper upon the record before us.

{Y}   [1] The judgment appealed from should be affirmed, with costs.

5.4 ANALYSIS OF *PALSGRAF V. LONG ISLAND RAILROAD*

✍ **A Note on the Approach Here**   Although our focus here is, once again, on the *reasoning* involved in the opinions of Justices Cardozo and Andrews, our approach to the analysis of the present case differs from that used for *Riggs*. Here we divide the analysis into three independent parts, each with its own goal, as follows:

Part I is preliminary and serves multiple purposes: it answers briefly some legally crucial elements such as facts, issue, and holding; it provides necessary background information for dealing more effectively with the complex text of the case; and it warns against some potential pitfalls that can easily sidetrack you in dealing with *Palsgraf.*

Part II engages in a thorough analysis of Justice Cardozo's majority opinion, very much in the manner of *Riggs*. There is a difference though: here our aim is to prompt you to engage in your own analysis, and so we shift the burden of discerning the judges' reasoning to you, the reader. Given the difficulty of the task, nonetheless, we provide you with some guidance both by posing some of the critical questions that need to be asked in order to analyze the reasoning in *Palsgraf,* as well as by providing our own "solution-answers" to these questions for your comparison. We suggest that you will benefit the most if you attempt to answer the suggested questions one at a time, making sure that you have a good understanding of the issue(s) involved before you proceed to the next question. Moreover, it is crucial that you tackle these questions in the order of their appearance, because the goal here is to *build* the main arguments a step at a time, and the order of the questions reflects that goal.

Part III deals with Judge Andrews's dissenting opinion. Our goal here is to provide you with a sample of "friendly analysis," an analysis that is closer to the interests of those who desire a more or less "bird's-eye overview" of the main points rather than a systematic and thorough dissection of every aspect of a judge's reasoning. We suggest that you will benefit the most from reading Part III if, prior to that reading, you have taken the following two steps in reverse order: (a) you have worked out your own summary overview of Judge Andrews's opinion, which you can compare to the one we provide; and (b) prior to working out your own summary, given that Judge Andrews's opinion centers on the relation of causality and the law, you have reread our discussion of that matter in section 3.3.3.2.

💣 **Caution**   We cannot overemphasize the fact that, due to the difficulty of the case, it must be read *several times* before any attempt to analyze any aspect of it is made.

Part I—Preliminaries

Facts   The facts of the case are stated quite clearly and succinctly by Judges Cardozo and Andrews respectively [**A1–11** and **H1–4**].

Procedural History and Judgment   Mrs. Palsgraf sued the Long Island Railroad, claiming that the negligent actions of its employees (the guards) caused her injuries, for which she sought compensation. At the trial the jury found that the defendant (or rather, the defendant's employees) was negligent, and Mrs. Palsgraf was awarded damages. When the railroad appealed the decision of the trial court, the appellate court found again for Mrs. Palsgraf and affirmed the judgment of the trial court. The case reached the New York Court of Appeals (the highest court in New York state), which reversed the judgment of the lower court in a 4–3 vote.

⚠ Torts and the Problem of the Unforeseeable Plaintiff   It should be clear that *Palsgraf* is an example of a *tort* claim, where one party who is injured (Mrs. Palsgraf) claims that the law should force another party (the railroad) to compensate her for her injuries, because these injuries were the result of *negligent* conduct (by the railroad's agents, the guards). Thus, this is a case about *tort liability for negligence* (Appendix II.1.3.1). Interestingly enough, however, the injury to Mrs. Palsgraf was not caused by the defendant's negligence *toward her,* but rather by the defendant's negligence *toward the carrier of the package with the explosives.* Moreover, given the particular facts of the case, it seems that the injury to Mrs. Palsgraf was not one that a reasonable person could have foreseen. Thus, what we have here is a case of X's (that is, the railroad's) negligence toward Y (that is, the passenger) that resulted in harm to a third party, Z (that is, Mrs. Palsgraf), a party who, in the eyes of a reasonable person, stood outside the area of any foreseeable danger. The problem here has come to be known as "the problem of the unforeseeable plaintiff," and *Palsgraf* has been the controlling case for *stare decisis* (section 3.3.3) in similar tort cases.

Issue   This can be put as follows: Can A's liability for negligent conduct toward B transfer to a third party C where (a) C sustained injuries as a result of A's conduct, and (b) these injuries could not have been reasonably foreseen? (*Holding:* A's liability for negligent conduct cannot transfer, and so on—see section 4.2.2.)

◆ False Starts   Given the complexity of the case, it is easy to become sidetracked and distracted by a number of potential "false starts"—points that are neither relevant nor helpful to the specific issues at stake in *Palsgraf.* Some of these points are made explicit and addressed in the following:

(1) Do not overlook the fact that *Palsgraf* is an *appellate* case, and the judges are being asked to decide *matters of law, not matters of fact* (Appendix II.2.2). That is, the appeals court here accepts the bare facts as established by the trial court, and so the important question before it is this: *Given* that the negligent conduct of the railroad employees caused the package to become dis-

lodged, and *given* that the package's becoming dislodged caused the package to fall and explode, and *given* that the explosion (or stampede) caused the scales to become dislodged, and (finally!) *given* that the falling scales caused Mrs. Palsgraf's injuries, should Mrs. Palsgraf be awarded compensation from the railroad for her injuries, since the negligent behavior of the railroad's employees caused Mrs. Palsgraf's injuries?

(2) Do not "point the finger" of fault at the passenger. You may be tempted to think that he should not have been carrying dangerous explosives, especially wrapped merely in newspaper, onto a passenger train, and therefore *he* rather than the railroad should be legally liable for Mrs. Palsgraf's injuries. Note that this point is not considered by the justices, and since they did not take the easy way out, we should be suspicious of easy answers.

(3) Do not think that the guards can be absolved of their wrongdoing because they were just "trying to help" the passenger. The fact that one is "just trying to help" does not necessarily absolve one from liability resulting from one's negligent behavior. (For instance, what would you make of the negligent physician's claim that he was "just trying to help" when he removed your healthy appendix instead of your ailing gallbladder?) What is more, the guards were not trying to help *Mrs. Palsgraf* at all—should the fact that they were trying to help the passenger entail that in so doing they cannot be found to be negligent toward Mrs. Palsgraf?

(4) Do not think that the guards did not act negligently, or that it was not their negligence that caused Mrs. Palsgraf's injuries. For whatever reason (it should not concern us), the jury at the trial court determined that the guards' conduct (in assisting the passenger) was negligent, and neither opinion of the appeals court challenges the issue. We must, therefore, assume with both justices that the guards' conduct was negligent. Moreover, each justice of the appeals court also agrees that it was this negligent conduct of the guards that caused Mrs. Palsgraf's injuries. And surely that is true at least in the sense that the guards' action satisfies the *but-for test* for determining the *cause-in-fact* (section 3.3.2): had the guards not been negligent, her injuries would not have occurred (or at least the injuries would not have occurred in the manner in which they did).

Part II—Questions and Answers on the Reasoning Involved in the Majority Opinion

Question 1   What exactly is the point of **B1–2**?

   Answer to Question 1   This is one of the main points of Judge Cardozo's written opinion. He claims that there is no such thing as negligence in the abstract ("negligence in the air"). Rather, negligence is always a *relative term;* it is always negligence *toward X.* Thus a person's act is not negligent *simpliciter,* but rather negligent *toward some specific person or persons.* This is important to Judge Cardozo, because he accepts that the guards *did* act negligently (and are thus liable for their act) and yet does not want to hold them liable for Mrs.

Palsgraf's injuries. A way to do this is to maintain that although the guards acted negligently, they did not act negligently *toward Mrs. Palsgraf.* So while their actions were negligent *toward the passenger,* insofar as they knocked his package from his grasp, they were not negligent *toward Mrs. Palsgraf.*

Question 2 What is the point of **B3**?

Answer to Question 2 The point here is clear enough: nothing in the appearance of the passenger's package could make a reasonable person suspect that it might conceal explosives about to cause harm to a person located far away (Mrs. Palsgraf). Although the point of this claim is quite clear, its appearance at this point in the text is problematic. Judge Cardozo needs the claim he makes at this juncture much later in order to complete his argument (see answer to question 4). But why does he present this claim just now? Is it just another example of an author who has little regard for making his argument clear or easy to the reader?

Question 3 What is the point of **B4–5**, and how is it argued?

Answer to Question 3 Here Judge Cardozo correlates *negligence* and *violation of a right.* Specifically, his claim that "negligence is not actionable unless . . ." translates as a *conditional* (section 1.3.2.3.1) to the effect that a *necessary condition* (section 1.3.2.3.2) for a negligent act to constitute a tort is that it results in a violation of a right. Thus, **B4** can be rewritten as:

(1) For an act to be negligent (toward person *P*), it is necessary that the act violates *P*'s rights.

Judge Cardozo substantiates (1) indirectly when in **B4** he uses an *authoritative legal source* (section 3.3.1) to the effect that there can be no negligence that does not satisfy the necessary condition posed in (1) (there can be no "negligence in the air"). It must be apparent in the context that Cardozo's specific concern is to establish that negligence on the part of the guards in this case must involve their violating one of Mrs. Palsgraf's rights.

Question 4 What are the subarguments, and what is the overall argument in **B6–10**?

Answer to Question 4 Here Judge Cardozo first specifies that the right allegedly violated in this case would be Mrs. Palsgraf's right to bodily security [**B6**]. Notice that given that much, claim (1) of the previous answer can now be rewritten for the specific case at hand as:

(1*) For the guards to have acted negligently toward Mrs. Palsgraf, it is necessary that their act has violated Mrs. Palsgraf's right to bodily security.

Though Judge Cardozo does not specifically state (1*), putting the issue this way will turn out to be useful in reconstructing the main argument.

Second, Mrs. Palsgraf's right to bodily security, Judge Cardozo tells us, is legally protected both against intentional invasions and against certain kinds of unintentional invasion [**B9**]. Given that no invasion of the former kind is charged (by Mrs. Palsgraf) [**B7**], we must conclude by *disjunctive syllogism* (section

2.4.2.1) that her (allegedly) violated right to bodily security was (allegedly) violated by the guards' act unintentionally. Thus, we can put the point that Judge Cardozo establishes here as follows:

> (2) If the guards' act has been a violation of Mrs. Palsgraf's right to bodily security, it has been an unintended violation (of that right).

Notice, however, that in **B8** Judge Cardozo adds an important qualification: Mrs. Palsgraf's right to bodily security is not protected against *every* act that constitutes an unintentional invasion of it but only against those acts "involving in the thoughts of reasonable men an unreasonable hazard that such invasion would ensue." Clearly, this is an important caveat. It means that one's right to bodily security is not unlimited. Rather, it is protected insofar as it is threatened by (unintentional) acts that would be perceived by "reasonable men" to involve "unreasonable hazard" that the right is to be violated. That is, perception of apparent harm by the "eye of ordinary vigilance," Justice Cardozo tells us [**B10**], is a *necessary condition* (section 1.3.2.3.2) for an unintended violation of one's right to bodily security to be a tort-wrong. And he reiterates the point in a *contrapositive* manner (section 1.3.3) in **B10** when he tells us that if no such hazard is perceived by a reasonably vigilant person, then we do not have an instance of a tort-wrong. With specific reference to Mrs. Palsgraf's right to bodily security then, we seem to have the following claim:

> (3) If the guards' act that constitutes an unintended violation of Mrs. Palsgraf's right to bodily security is to be a tort-wrong, it is necessary that it be such that it can be perceived in the eyes of reasonable persons as one that has the risk of harming *her.*

Put this way, we can now see that the stage for the defeat of Mrs. Palsgraf's case has been set: all that Judge Cardozo needs now is the claim that no reasonable person could have foreseen that knocking an innocent looking newspaper-wrapped bundle would result in violation of *Mrs. Palsgraf's* right to bodily security. And, indeed, he makes such a claim—unfortunately much earlier, in **B3.**

Let us see now if we can reconstrue Judge Cardozo's extremely compressed argument in **B3–10** with regard to the guards' alleged violation of Mrs. Palsgraf's right to bodily security. When we take the claim presented in **B3** in the text along with proposition (3), we can conclude by *modus tollens* (section 2.4.2.1) that:

> (i) The guards' act that constitutes an unintended violation of Mrs. Palsgraf's right to bodily security is not a tort-wrong toward Mrs. Palsgraf.

So far, so good. But how do we get from this to the apparent overall conclusion of this segment that the guards did not act negligently toward Mrs. Palsgraf? One way to do this is to utilize the newly arrived proposition (i) along with the following suppressed claim:

(4) If there has been an unintended violation of Mrs. Palsgraf's right to bodily security, the unintended violation must have been a tort-wrong toward Mrs. Palsgraf.

Then, by modus tollens, (4) along with (i) yield the conclusion:

(ii) There has not been an unintended violation of Mrs. Palsgraf's right to bodily security.

When we look back, we realize that Judge Cardozo has argued for the truth of claims (1*) and (2). But when we take propositions (1*) and (2) together, we can conclude by *hypothetical syllogism* (section 2.4.2.1) that:

(iii) For the guards to have acted negligently toward Mrs. Palsgraf, it is necessary that their act has been an unintended violation of Mrs. Palsgraf's right to bodily security.

Given that much, we can now take (ii) and (iii) together and derive, by modus tollens, the final conclusion that:

(iv) The guards have not acted negligently toward Mrs. Palsgraf.

Question 5   What does Judge Cardozo establish in **B11–13**?

Answer to Question 5   So far, Judge Cardozo has approached the matter from the perspective of Mrs. Palsgraf's *rights,* specifically her right to bodily security. But to Mrs. Palsgraf's right to bodily security corresponds the guards' duty not to violate it. Thus, Judge Cardozo also tackles the issue from the perspective of *duties owed* by the guards to Mrs. Palsgraf. He announces that there is a "correlation" between negligence and duty and supports his claim by appealing to precedent [**B12**]. And he appeals to precedent once more to establish that the specific nature of the correlation is this: a necessary condition for an act to be negligent *toward an individual P* is that there is a *duty to P* ("to the individual complaining") that the act violated [**B11**]. A couple of observations are in order.

First, notice that with these claims, Judge Cardozo, once again, relativizes the negligence–duty correlation: if Mrs. Palsgraf's claim that the guards acted negligently *toward her* is to be legally sustainable, one must identify some *duty to Mrs. Palsgraf* with which the guards failed to comply, and which, if they had complied with it, would have prevented the injuries *to her.*

Second, just what is the point of **B13** at this juncture? The answer is that Judge Cardozo now points out that this is *not* a case where one is complaining *on behalf of someone else* (as it might have been, for example, if the package-carrying passenger was fatally injured and the suit was brought against the railroad by his widow). Rather, Mrs. Palsgraf's suit against the railroad is for injuries sustained *personally by her.* Thus, in view of what Judge Cardozo has established in **B11–12**, he can now claim that Mrs. Palsgraf can show that the guards acted negligently (toward her) *only if* (section 1.3.2.3.1) they have violated *a duty owed to her.* He establishes, that is, the following crucial claim:

(5) For the guards to have acted negligently toward Mrs. Palsgraf, it is necessary that they have violated a duty owed to her.

At this point, if Judge Cardozo can further establish the missing claim that the guards did not violate any duties owed to Mrs. Palsgraf, then he can validly conclude (by modus tollens) that, even from the perspective of duties owed to Mrs. Palsgraf, the guards still did not act negligently toward her. He needs, that is, the following missing premise:

(6) The guards have not violated a duty owed to Mrs. Palsgraf.

Of course, this missing claim is not obvious, and Judge Cardozo needs to establish it.

Question 6 What does Judge Cardozo establish in **C1–11**?

Answer to Question 6 In **C1–6**, Judge Cardozo first presents us with a compact line of reasoning that could be used to justify the truth of claim (6) (see answer to question 5). Mrs. Palsgraf's case of having suffered a violation of her right to bodily security is based on (is derived from), Judge Cardozo tells us, the guards' violation of a *different* (and presumably minor) right *of someone else,* namely, the property right of the passenger. But how can it be, Judge Cardozo wonders, that the violation of right *X* owed to person *A* counts as a violation of a different right *Y* owed to a different person *B*? To put the same thing in terms of duties: if there was a violation of a duty owed by the guards, that was a violation of a duty owed *to the passenger,* namely, their duty to take due care to *protect his property* interests (that is, the safety of his package); but Mrs. Palsgraf's claim is based on the guards' violation of a duty of a *different order,* namely, their duty to take due care not to violate *her bodily security.* But how can this latter duty be *derived* from the former? And if not, in what sense did the guards violate a duty owed to Mrs. Palsgraf? In the end, the conclusion that seems to be forced upon us from these considerations is that, as claim (6) has it, the guards did not violate a duty owed to Mrs. Palsgraf after all.

Notice, however, that Judge Cardozo does not want to make much of the present "diversity of interests" line of reasoning. Instead he treats it as *dicta* (section 3.4.2) by telling us that his point here "is one of emphasis" [**C7**], and he moves on to establish a different point, a point about the limits of the guards' duty to Mrs. Palsgraf. These limits, Judge Cardozo tells us in **C8,** are defined in terms of a reasonable person's ability to perceive the risks that would ensue had that duty been violated. More simply put, the guards, and indeed all of us in society, have a duty to avoid those actions that carry a risk of harm to others that would be perceived by (as Justice Cardozo puts it) the "eye of ordinary vigilance," that is, the perceptions of the familiar "reasonable person." It follows that, minimally, the violation of the duty of the guards toward Mrs. Palsgraf would have taken place subject to the satisfaction of a *necessary condition* as follows:

(7) For the guards to have violated their duty to Mrs. Palsgraf, it is *necessary* that the eye of ordinary vigilance could have perceived the risks that would have ensued from the violation of that duty.

A couple of questions should emerge at this point: (a) why does Judge Cardozo present us with this claim here? and (b) why should we believe that it is true? The answer to the first question is rather straightforward: Judge Cardozo is still working to present us with a fairly uncontroversial line of reasoning in support of his crucial claim (6) earlier. Presumably he must feel that the "diversity of interests" line of reasoning before is not fruitful. By contrast, there is an easier, straightforward way to establish (6): if we have claim (7), then along with a relatively uncontroversial claim to the effect that no reasonable person could have perceived the dangers here, claim (6) would be established as the conclusion of a valid modus tollens. Thus claim (7) is an important one for Justice Cardozo's overall argument. The answer to the second question is more complicated. Apparently Judge Cardozo gives us a reason to believe (7) when he provides a subargument in its support in **C9–11**. Unfortunately, despite its deceptive brevity and simplicity, his reasoning here involves a complex argumentative technique that will take us too far afield to explore. So we will keep it simple: we should believe (7), Judge Cardozo seems to be saying, since *if we did not* this would amount to (a) setting a legal standard for behavior to which no human could conform, that is, that people are to be held liable for results that they could not possibly foresee (the suppressed premise being that we should not do that), and (b) imposing wholesale changes in how society demands that we deal with each other (and we ought not to do that either).

Question 7 What is Judge Cardozo's argument in **D1–11**?

Answer to Question 7 Judge Cardozo's apparent goal here is to complete the argument he started earlier with regard to the guards' not being negligent on account of having violated their duties. He achieves his goal in stages. As a first step [**D1–7**], consistent with his overall approach to negligence, he clarifies that the notion of risk perceived by the eye of ordinary vigilance is *relative:* there can be no such thing as "perceived risk at large." Even when we may be tempted to think otherwise (for example, in the case of "one who drives with reckless speed through a crowded city street" [**D3**]), risk is always *risk perceived relative to specific person(s)* [**D6**]. Given that much, it follows that the appropriate proposition here is not (7), but rather the more precisely formulated (7*):

> (7*) For the guards to have violated their duty *to Mrs. Palsgraf*, it is *necessary* that the eye of ordinary vigilance could have perceived the risks *to her* that would have ensued from the violation of that duty.

The second and final step that Judge Cardozo takes here [**D8–11**] is to assert that no reasonable person could have anticipated that the dropping of the innocent-looking package would have resulted in harm to Mrs. Palsgraf who was standing far away. Indeed, Judge Cardozo tells us, nothing in the appearance of the passenger's package could have made even a "most cautious mind" suspect that there was a probability that it "would spread wreckage through the station" and cause bodily harm to Mrs. Palsgraf if it was dropped (either accidentally or intentionally). That is, the following claim seems to be true:

(8) The eye of ordinary vigilance could *not* have perceived the risks *to Mrs. Palsgraf* that would have ensued from the guards' violation of their duty to her.

Question 8 What is Judge Cardozo's overall argument from **B11–D11**?

Answer to Question 8 In this segment of his opinion, Judge Cardozo argues overall that even from the perspective of *duties owed* by the guards to Mrs. Palsgraf, the guards did not act negligently toward her. In summary, his argument is this: From (7*) and (8) (see answer to question 7), we can conclude by modus tollens that proposition (6) (see answer to question 5) is true. But from (6) along with (5) (see answer to question 5), we can conclude by modus tollens that the following proposition (9) is true:

(9) The guards have not acted negligently toward Mrs. Palsgraf.

Notice that this is the same conclusion as the one Judge Cardozo reached when he examined the possibility of the guards' negligence (toward Mrs. Palsgraf) from the perspective of the possible violation of Mrs. Palsgraf's right to bodily security.

Question 9 What is the goal of Judge Cardozo's final remarks in **E1–F3**?

Answer to Question 9 In this final part of his opinion, Judge Cardozo provides a threefold summary of the crucial points of his decision. First, he reiterates the central claims that have played a decisive role in the course of his argument [**E1–7**]. Second, he brings out explicitly the guiding perspective of his opinion, namely, the view that conclusions as to negligence should not be derived on the basis of causal considerations [**F1**]. (We need to turn to Justice Andrews's opinion to fully understand this.) Finally, he derives the logical consequence of his conclusion that the guards did not act negligently toward Mrs. Palsgraf: a necessary condition for assessing liability for damages to Mrs. Palsgraf is that we have found that the guards have acted negligently toward her; since, as it has been shown, there was no negligence here, we can conclude (by modus tollens) that there is no question of liability here either.

Part IIII—Summary Overview of Justice Andrews's Dissent

The conclusion of Justice Andrews's argument is that the railroad is liable for Mrs. Palsgraf's injuries, and therefore she is owed compensation for them. Since the two justices agree that the railroad was negligent toward the passenger but disagree as to whether liability for their negligence extends to Mrs. Palsgraf's injuries, and they agree as well that negligence involves the violation of a right, we may assume that Justice Andrews believes that the railroad violated Mrs. Palsgraf's right to bodily security. And, indeed, that is exactly what he claims. But then Justice Andrews must believe that the right to bodily security protects us against more than just those injuries that would be foreseen by the eye of ordinary vigilance. Indeed, the central component of Justice Andrews's reasoning is the claim that *the right to bodily security covers all injuries that are the "proximate result" of negligent conduct,* and that if one acts negligently, one's liability extends to *all* injuries of which the negligent conduct is the "proximate cause." As such, Justice Andrews must establish two points: (a) a defense of the "proximate cause" standard for tort liability, and (b) a showing that Mrs. Palsgraf's injuries were the "proximate result" of the guards' negligent conduct.

With regard to the issue of the legal standard for liability, Justice Andrews argues that if the standard is "what can reasonably be foreseen," liability would depend on a fairly complicated calculation of probability of harm, whereas if the issue is one of proximate cause, one needs only to determine cause and effect. The point here is that the "reasonable forseeability" criterion would require a cumbersome, controversial, and perhaps indeterminate judgment. (Who is doing the "foreseeing"—an engineer, a plumber, a cab driver? And exactly how much information does this person have about the situation—does she know about the fireworks, the precariously perched scales or the location of Mrs. Palsgraf?)

Further, the account suggested by Justice Cardozo is too narrow. Though it may well be that negligence consists of failure to exercise due care, and that negligent acts must (in order to result in liability) affect the rights of others, the correct view, Judge Andrews argues, is that our duty to due care "is imposed on each of us to protect society from unnecessary danger, not just to protect A, B or C alone." The point is that Justice Cardozo's conception is too narrow—for example, speeding is not just negligent toward those who are actually in the path of the speeding vehicle, it is negligent toward "all those who might have been there"—to the "public at large." And even though there is no negligence in the abstract, negligence involves violating the duty not to injure those who the negligent act *actually injures.* So this is how it works: We have a duty to everyone to exercise due care, and when we fail to do so and injuries result, we have breached the specific duty *owed to those who we actually injure.* In that way, Justice Andrews believes he can avoid the "negligence in the air" difficulty while maintaining that causation, not forseeability of harm, provides the criterion for liability. He also believes that legal precedent supports his position (in *Polemis,* it was held that performance of a wrongful act entails liability for its proximate results). So according to Justice Andrews, when a negligent act is performed and harm occurs, the wronged parties might include not only those whose injuries might reasonably be expected, but those whose injuries were caused by the negligent conduct, even if they were out of the "danger zone" circumscribed by the eye of ordinary vigilance.

For legal liability to be incurred for injuries caused by negligent conduct, all that is needed is that the injuries be the "proximate result" of the conduct—even if the injuries were unexpected, unforeseen, or unforeseeable. While Justice Andrews admits that determining when a causal relation is "proximate" enough to result in legal liability is a difficult issue, he argues that it is certainly no worse in that respect than the "eye of ordinary vigilance" and "reasonable expectation." He argues that for the purpose of determining liability, the courts will trace causality only so far back through the (presumably infinite) series of prior causes.

The point at which tort law stops and says "that is as far back as liability extends" is to be determined, Justice Andrews claims, by "practical politics" as opposed to logic. The courts ask questions about whether the causal relation between the negligent conduct and the injury is "direct and local," and whether there are too many intervening causes (that is why remoteness is space and time matters). One important consideration is whether there are any voluntary, deliberate human actions interposed between the negligent conduct and the injury within the causal chain. Presumably, liability for injuries caused by one's negligent conduct ends at the point where some other deliberate, voluntary action provides a necessary link in the causal chain.

Consider how this would apply in the hypothetical case that Justice Andrews introduces. In this case we are asked to imagine that a chauffeur collides with a vehicle containing dynamite. Suppose that the chauffeur's negligence caused the collision, that the owner/operator of the other vehicle is without fault, and that the explosion causes injuries. Specifically, *A* is killed on the sidewalk next to the collision, *B* is injured in a building on the opposite side of the street, *C* is hurt by flying glass a block away, and ten blocks away, a nanny is startled by the explosion and drops an infant that she is carrying. Well, who is owed compensation by the negligent chauffeur? Justice Andrews argues that the chauffeur should make good every injury that "flowed from" (or was the "natural result" of) his negligent conduct. But how far do we trace the consequences? Justice Andrews tacitly assumes that the right approach is not to enlist the eye of ordinary vigilance or to calculate the probability of each specific injury, but instead to reason in terms of cause and effect (he later says that they should each recover, especially if the explosion really did startle the nanny, and that she was not behaving negligently and did not deliberately drop the infant), and to determine whether the relationship between the negligence and the injury is one of proximate cause.

Now back to Mrs. Palsgraf. Justice Andrews argues that "injury in some form" (at the very least to the passenger's package) was the likely result of the guards' negligence. So if she were standing next to the car where the explosion occurred, and she were hurt by the explosion itself, her injuries would undoubtedly be compensated. But as a matter of fact she was located about twenty-five or thirty feet from the actual explosion. Clearly she would not have been injured had the explosion not occurred. And the only intervening cause in the causal chain that started with the explosion and ended with her injuries was the rattling and dislodging of the scales. The relationship between the negligence and her injuries was not remote in space and time, and there was certainly no intermediate cause in the form of a deliberate, voluntary human action. Injury in some form was probable from the negligence, even though the specific type of injury that Mrs. Palsgraf sustained might not have been either probable or foreseeable. But since the causal relation is direct enough, Justice Andrews concludes that the railroad should be forced to pay compensation to Mrs. Palsgraf for her injuries.

TO THINK ABOUT

(1) Suppose that the Long Island Railroad, the defendant in this case, had postulated the following as a rule:

> Employees should make every effort to assist people to embark on trains. If a train is not at a complete stop at the station, employees should use their discretion in assisting people to embark.

How would this rule influence the case?

(2) It should be recalled that Judge Cardozo dismissed Mrs. Palsgraf's complaint "with costs." That made Mrs. Palsgraf responsible for all the legal expenses that her case incurred in the courts (including compensating the railroad company for their costs). It has been observed that she was a woman of modest means and that her legal bills amounted to about $350, a sum that was about equal to what she was making in a year; by contrast, the railroad company was a thriving business with assets of more than $1.5 billion. Should this information have made any difference?

(3) Judges Cardozo and Andrews disagree on the correct theory of negligence, and hold "opposite" theories. Can you summarize the main tenets of their respective theories? Can you evaluate the pros and cons of each theory?

GUIDELINES FOR WRITING ARGUMENTATIVE PAPERS

BEFORE YOU START WRITING

Before you begin, keep in mind that there are (at least) two prerequisites for success in this context; namely, you must (a) be clear as to the unique perspective involved here, and (b) have the right attitude.

Perspective: Argue Your Case

It is of paramount importance to realize from the start that the main goal of an analytical-argumentative paper is to *rationally convince* your reader that you are right in the claims you make. Thus the emphasis must be on justification, on the *arguments* you provide to support your claims. There are three immediate consequences that emerge from understanding the unique perspective of argumentative papers:

- Be critical and confrontational. Do not passively accept facts, opinions, and arguments.
- Be analytical. Think "detail," and avoid broad, sweeping generalizations and "comprehensive pictures" of the whole subject.
- Be original. Present *your* arguments, and do not report back the facts and/or the views and arguments of others.

Attitude: Win Your Case

Oceans of literature speak of a direct and indisputable correlation between positive attitude and success. This correlation applies here too: to have a successful argumentative paper, you need to have the right attitude about writing it. What attitude? If you reflect for a moment on what has been said about the peculiar nature of an analytical-argumentative paper, it will become clear that writing this sort of paper is a problem-solving activity: you are given a puzzle, and you are challenged to come up with a solution. This is a demanding, challenging task. But it is also fun if you confront it as a "game," and it is quite rewarding if you win. The suggestion then is this: engage in the writing of your paper as if it is a game, and "play" to win. The results you will get from adopting this sort of attitude will be by far better than those you will get from adopting the opposite "oh-so-many-pages-to-be-filled-by-tomorrow" attitude.

> 💣 **Caution**   At any stage of the writing process of your paper, do not lose sight of the perspective and the attitude involved here.

WRITING THE PAPER

There are many ways you can go about writing a good argumentative paper, but the simplest one involves taking the following three steps:

1. Thinking before leaping
2. Writing a draft
3. Rewriting the paper

In what follows, you will find some basic issues that are involved in taking these steps.

Step 1—Thinking before Leaping

This is the most important phase of the writting process. There are three closely interrelated things you should do at this stage of the game.

(1a) Narrow Down

If a specific topic has already been assigned to you, you are in luck: choosing a topic that you can adequately handle in a limited number of pages is not easy, since the usual temptation is to engage in a broad project. If it is up to you to select a topic, choose one that interests you, but be careful: make sure that the subject or problem that you choose is small enough to handle within the required number of pages. If you find yourself struggling with the paper, your biggest problem may well be that you have overextended yourself.

(1b) "Research" the Topic

Argumentative papers primarily involve original, critical analysis of a narrow topic rather than "looking-up-and-reporting" what has already been said on the subject. Thus, "research" in the usual sense of collecting and citing data from materials found in the library should not be the primary activity in the process of writing the paper.

This is not to say, however, that you should not consult any published materials. Reading from the source materials those portions that relate to your topic gives you the background you need in order to understand better the issues and main problems involved in your topic. In sum, it is fine to do research as long as you use it *as a springboard for your own ideas.*

(1c) Reflect before You Write

Think about what you want to accomplish. Examine the basic statements of the position or topic you have chosen; determine what they mean, and ask whether they seem to be true or not. If you decide that they are not true, try to figure out why they are not true.

Step 2—Writing a Draft

(2a) Starting Techniques

If you believe that you can produce a decent argumentative paper in the first draft, you are probably wrong. Writers who have this extraordinary ability are very rare; the average writer should expect to rewrite several times. If you belong to the first category, you might as well stop reading this, for you do not need it. If you are like the rest of us, read on.

There are several ways in which you could go about starting your draft, and no single one fits everyone best. Here are two basic ones:

- *The Argument—First Way:* Think of a single main point you want to make and of the main reasons you have for believing that it is true. Write this down as a "skeleton argument" (where your point is the conclusion and the reasons are the premises). Repeat this process with the next main point, the third, and so on. When you start organizing your paper, you will expand on these skeleton-arguments to construct your full paper.
- *The Brainstorm—Second Way:* Write down whatever comes to mind when you think about the subject, and pay no attention to the order or organization of your ideas. As a next step, go through what you have written, pick any points that seem worth pursuing, and examine whether these points can be proven soundly. If not, rework them. If necessary, repeat this process.

(2b) Organizing the Paper

You need to have (i) an introduction, (ii) a conclusion, and (iii) a main body. The first two are the easy parts so let us deal with them first.

The Introduction   Since an argumentative paper is concerned with problems, begin your paper with a statement of the specific problem or issue you are dealing with. Sometimes, beginning with a specific question achieves the "narrowing down" we discussed earlier and gives you direction. A couple of crucial "dos" and "don'ts" for the introduction:

Do

Make sure that you state as clearly and succinctly as you can what you will attempt to accomplish in your paper. Always include a "goal statement" of the form "In this paper, I will argue (show, attempt to prove) that. . . ." If you wish, you can follow your goal statement with a summary of the plan of the paper (an overview of the main points you will elaborate on). This is always welcomed by the reader, since it gives directions as to what one should be looking for in the course of the reading. So do it, but be specific and to the point.

Don't

Do not write long and obscure introductions, and do not attempt to impress your reader with "nice literary sentences." Chances are that this will backfire: you will end up with a critical comment to the effect that you use obscure language, or generalities, or irrelevancies. If you want to impress the reader of an argumentative paper, concentrate on your arguments.

The Conclusion If you have made good points along the way, your reader knows it. And if your arguments are not all that good, there is not much the conclusion can do to repair them. So keep your concluding remarks brief and to the point. So what should the conclusion be all about? There is no single recipe, but here are a few suggestions:

Do

First, if your paper reaches a conclusion (a "discovery" of sorts), you should provide a very quick summary/reminder of your main points showing how they lead to this conclusion (for example, "Based upon the criticisms that I have made, we can conclude that. . . ." Second, if your paper does not arrive at a definite solution, you should provide pointers to the areas, problems, and questions that need to be explored further in order to resolve the issue you have examined.

Don't

First, do not repeat at length what you have just said in the main body of your text. If you say more than the minimum necessary to trigger your reader's memory in regard to the main points you have made, you run the risk of insulting your reader's intelligence. Second, do not end your paper with an abrupt, sudden stop. This indicates to the reader that you have not made the effort to acquire a comprehensive overview of the subject you are addressing.

The Main Body In general, the content of the main body of your paper should consist of careful and detailed arguments. However, there are two complications here. The first complication is that arguing effectively is a skill that one develops through time by learning and practicing methods and techniques of arguing. The second complication is that, apart from length considerations, analytical-argumentative papers come in several kinds. Without attempting to be exhaustive, we can distinguish: (a) purely critical papers—in these you provide no positive thesis of your own, but you adopt a confrontational attitude against a position and the arguments offered in support of that position; (b) purely positive papers—in these you bring forth a positive thesis and you "build" that thesis with arguments that aim to support it; (c) mixed papers—in these you attempt a combination of (a) and (b); and (d) exploratory papers—in these you provide arguments and analysis that form a "map of the logical territory of the area," and you do not necessarily reach a conclusion of your own. Given that much, the best that can be done here is to point out some essential dos and don'ts that cut across all argumentative papers.

Do

Follow the prime rule: *show it (argue it), do not just say it.* Beyond this, the following are desirable procedures that should be taken into consideration:

- *State clearly:* (1) the major claims being made and the questions at issue. In stating the positions involved as clearly and fairly as possible, you will understand them better, and you will avoid the risk of talking at cross-purposes; and (2) the meaning of the central terms involved. Ask yourself, "Are all key terms used clearly, or are some ambiguous, vague, or even meaningless?"

- *Analyze:* (1) the logic of your position and that of the opposing position. Attempt to give *good* reasons for your own position and *good* reasons against the position you oppose; (2) the assumptions being made by a position (what does it take for granted?); and (3) the implications of a position (could it lead to a contradiction, to a falsity?).

- *Use concrete examples:* examples help illustrate what you want to express. Your goal is to persuade, and common day-to-day examples are powerful tools of persuasion.

- *Put yourself in a possible opponent's shoes:* try to imagine how an opponent might respond to what you are saying. This may be difficult to do, but its importance cannot be overemphasized. It is never enough to provide *some* arguments for a claim and leave the issue there. Arguments are about controversial claims, and thus there will always be those who think differently than you on the issue at hand. If your opponent can easily dismiss your arguments, what is the persuasive value of your arguments? Always play devil's advocate and try to anticipate what may be forthcoming from the opposite camp. In argumentation, you always play to win.

Don't

- Do not uncritically rely on an alleged authority. Simply because someone claims that X is true does not mean that it is true.

- Do not use obscure and figurative language. Avoid generalities and expressions that are used to impress rather than to rationally convince.

- Do not assume that your reader is familiar with what you say. Explain the positions and problem(s) to your reader. A good test is to read what you have written to someone of your intellectual level who is unfamiliar with your topic and see if he/she understands the issues and the arguments from what you are saying in your paper.

- Do not attempt to do too much in the limited space of a paper. It is best to deal with one argument and examine it as thoroughly as you can rather than attempt to provide a series of "argumentative considerations," none of which is pursued in any depth.

- Do not use a single paragraph to discuss distinct, unrelated points and arguments.

Step 3—Rewriting the Paper

This may seem like a time-consuming process, and you may feel that you could skip it. However, it is a crucial part of the paper, as the following imply:

Do

- Check the strength of your *arguments.* There is no single rule on how to do this. You can try the following:

    —Omit weak, unreliable, and hastily presented arguments. As has been already mentioned, it is best to have a few good and detailed arguments than a series of hasty "proofs."

    —Fill gaps in the arguments you keep. Often you have assumed too much, and you have not given enough substantiation for the truth of crucial claims you have made. Omit expressions like "it is clear," "it is obvious," and the like.

    —Clarify your claims. Rephrase obscure sentences with ones that employ specific and clear language. Rephrase strong, disrespectful language.

- Check the *organization* of your material. Make sure that your paper does not look like a shopping list, a series of "and another thing. . . ." Put distinct arguments in separate paragraphs, and attempt to provide a smooth transition from one issue to another.

- Check your *grammar.* At this stage, make sure that your paper is free of mechanical errors. Misspellings, misprints, lack of reasonable neatness, and incomplete sentences are things that can only hurt you. Use a dictionary.

- Check the *documentation* of your sources. Acknowledge properly your sources. Plagiarism is a serious offense, and you should stay clear of generating a suspicion of it in your reader. Use a standard manual of style (for example, *The MLA Handbook*), and follow the directions.

💣 **Caution**   Do not skip the rewriting phase. After all the effort you have put into the paper, it is nonsensical to give away half the value of it. This is, in effect, what you do when you do not take this final step!

APPENDIX II

LEGAL FUNDAMENTALS

II.1 THE NATURE OF LAW

The question of *legal validity,* that is, the question of what is to count as a genuinely true law (within a particular legal system), has puzzled philosophers and legal theorists for centuries. To be sure, the ordinary person will find the question "What is law?" rather strange and inconsequential. (Most people are able to recognize specific laws and distinguish them from such nonlaws as, for example, rules of chess or baseball.). Yet legal theorists find that questions about the nature of law raise a variety of interesting and difficult issues. Thus, for example, legal theorists note with great interest the fact that a judge's own understanding of the nature of law affects the way new law is created: in every single case that comes in front of a judge, the judge's own conception of the nature of law colors how she interprets the relevant law(s) in the case. This, in turn, affects her decision regarding what will be the law in that case! But we are now moving ahead into deeply theoretical territory. Thus, we must take a very brief bird's-eye look at the two main rival currents or perspectives in addressing the issue of legal validity, namely, *naturalism* and *positivism.*

Legal Naturalism   This is the view that the idea of valid law is best explained by reference to a set of objective *moral* principles or truths that exist in nature. Properly understood, valid law consists of a set of true rules that conform to ideals of human perfectibility and what counts as a "good life" for humans. Typically, naturalists try to discover a set of ideal rules or standards that will enable people to live in harmony, secure justice, and achieve a state of well-being. The law is an important social instrument whose purpose is to bring about such a state. So, *all and only those rules that conform to these standards are valid law.* Exercises of legal coercion that violate these standards are not law at all—they are instances of violence.

Naturalism has deep roots in human intellectual thought. Thus, for example, the ancient Greeks explicitly admitted the existence of natural laws (for example, in Sophocles's *Antigone,* the protagonist proclaims that she is not going to disobey "the great unwritten, unshakable traditions . . . [that] live forever"); the Stoics postulated a moral order in the universe; and the Roman jurists introduced the notion of *jus naturalis* as an integral part their highly developed legal framework. In the Middle Ages, St. Thomas Aquinas developed one of the most elegant versions of naturalism by arguing that there is an objective teleological morality that should be self-evident to anyone who is minimally rational and has given sufficient thought to the issue.

Despite its appeal, naturalism has not been without its problems. One set of difficulties facing the view has to do with identifying and justifying a set of objective moral truths or standards to which valid law must conform. The naturalist faces the challenge that conscientious people often disagree about exactly what counts as a "good life" (Aquinas thought it was "living according to God's will"). Moreover, even when they do agree about what a good life is (healthy, secure, relatively free, and so on), they may still disagree about which set of rules is best suited to enable us to achieve this end (for example, does it include national health insurance?). So not only are the naturalist's goals, and the rules that would lead us there, not self-evident, but they are highly controversial among even the most reasonable and conscientious thinkers on the subject. And if, as the naturalist claims, valid laws must adhere to standards that are derived from these goals and rules, virtually all claims of legal validity would be controversial and perhaps even unsolvable. As if this were not bad enough, all debates about legal validity, even on relatively minor issues, would degenerate into debates about difficult philosophical issues, such as the nature of the good life (does it really require that tax returns be filed by the 15th of April?).

Legal Positivism   This can best be viewed as an attempt to address some of the more serious difficulties facing naturalism. This view is called legal "positivism" because its fundamental tenet is that legal validity is a matter of a rule's *position,* that is, its origins. The ideal behind positivism is that we should view legal systems as empirical phenomena whose central concepts such as "valid law" do not require delving into deep philosophical and metaphysical issues such as the nature of the good life. For the positivist, the law is a set of rules that has come into existence in a particular way. The great positivist pioneer John Austin argued that laws are essentially commands, that is, orders backed up by threats. But only the commands of a legal "sovereign" (one who is habitually obeyed and habitually obeys no one) are valid laws. Not all positivists share Austin's views on commands and sovereignty, but they do share the contention that *legal validity is a function of the origin of a rule, so that valid laws are rules that have come into existence "in the right way."* This is indeed a core feature of legal positivism.

A second core feature of legal positivism is related to the first. If legal validity is merely a function of a rule's origins, then it would seem to follow that there is no restriction on the specific content that a valid law might have. But if there is no restriction on the content of valid law, according to the positivists, there can be no requirement of moral content for a law to be valid. This is known as the *separability thesis—that there is no necessary connection between law and morality.* This contrasts starkly with naturalism, which holds that there is an intimate connection between law and morality—indeed, that no rule that has immoral content could ever be valid law, whatever its origins. A quick example will illustrate the point. Suppose that within a specific legal system, the proper origin of valid law is that it be ordered by the king (approximating Austin's "command of a sovereign"). Now suppose that the king orders the execution of all male newborn babies of a specific minority group that lives within his land. Since this order satisfies the appropriate "pedigree" requirement, it is valid law as far as positivism goes; since it has an essentially immoral content, however, it cannot be a valid law in the eyes of the naturalists.

The rivalry between naturalism and positivism is very much alive and well. Recent scholarship in legal theory has included two sophisticated versions of the positivist and naturalist views. H.L.A. Hart argues for a version of positivism that includes the separability thesis and a sophisticated version of the "right origin" criterion of legal validity. Briefly, Hart argues that valid laws are those whose origins conform to the standards of what he calls a rule of recognition. But he also argues that in some cases, judges must reach outside these rules in making their decisions. This aspect of Hart's view has led Ronald Dworkin to argue for what some view as a version of legal naturalism. Dworkin argues that in deciding hard cases, judges must employ *principles* that have an essential *moral* content, and whose legal status cannot be demonstrated by any positivistic rule of recognition. Although some have argued that Dworkin's view really is not naturalistic after all, it is worth noting that the status of positivism and naturalism plays a central role in contemporary debate in legal theory.

We should briefly point out that there are hints of both naturalistic and positivistic thought in the most fundamental defining documents of the American legal system. For instance, in the Declaration of Independence, we find the claim that "We hold these truths as self-evident that all men are created equal and endowed by their Creator with rights to life, liberty and the pursuit of happiness." Likewise, the U.S. Constitution contains claims that the purpose and justification for the union is to "secure justice" and "provide for the general welfare." These are clearly naturalistic aims, and it would appear legitimate to infer that no valid law could conflict with these provisions. Yet, on the other hand, the American system also allows that any bill passed by a majority of both houses of Congress and signed by the president is valid law, and that the Constitution itself can be amended by a combined congressional vote and a supermajority of the legislatures of the states. These provisions are positivistic in disavowing any content-based test for validity, and specifying a precise origin for valid law. The moral here is that it would be a mistake to look within these sorts of documents for conclusive evidence favoring either the naturalists or the positivists.

II.1.1 Sources of Law: Statutory and Case Law

An important issue that faces the student of law is the issue of what exactly are the sources of law. The answer to this may be a bit more complicated than it may at first seem, but for the sake of simplicity, we can say that the American legal system recognizes three main authoritative sources of law: *constitutional provisions, statutes,* and *cases.* Constitutional provisions, naturally, appear in either the U.S. or state constitutions. Statutory laws are the products of a legislative authority (national, state, or local) that enacts laws in conformity with a set of appropriate procedures. State and federal penal codes, state commercial codes, and tax codes are examples of statutes.

Case law results from the decisions of courts. As we will see in section II.2.2, decisions of trial courts are often appealed on a point of law to a higher level court, an appellate court. Appellate courts authoritatively decide the controversy at hand, and their decisions set a precedent that has the *force of law* for the resolution of future cases within its jurisdiction that are similar to the one they have decided. The process and function of case law is quite fundamental in the American legal system and merits close attention.

The Common Law System

The United States legal system is a *common law system.* This is a system of law that developed in England long ago when king-appointed judges decided cases brought before them without the aid of written codes or statutes. Their decision *was the law* and became *precedent* for deciding later cases with similar facts. The common law system is prevalent to this day in English-speaking countries and is contrasted with systems of law that are primarily dependent on written codes (*civil law systems*), which purport to exhaustively anticipate and answer the legal issues that may come before a judge. In the United States, large areas of the law (such as contracts, property, and torts) are largely dominated by common law.

II.1.2 Private and Public Law—Civil and Criminal Law

The American legal system is traditionally subdivided in the following way: (1) *private versus public* law, and (2) *civil versus criminal* law. Although there is a great deal of controversy among legal scholars about these commonly employed distinctions, we skip that debate here and confine our discussion to a brief consideration of the "common sense" understanding of these terms.

II.1.2.1 Private Interests and State Interests: Private Law versus Public Law

Private Law   This is the realm in which the law deals with interactions between individuals as private citizens in the legal system. That is, in the area of private law, the legal issues that arise are always between two or more parties, neither of whom is acting as an official law enforcement arm of the government. Matters such as *family law, estates,* and (as we shall see in the following) *torts* and *contracts* are typical subjects for private law proceedings.

Public Law   This is the domain of law that involves such matters as the fundamental principles on which a particular society is founded (*constitutional* *law*); rules set by a governmental agency to regulate the actions of special groups, for example, businesses or taxpayers (*administrative law*); procedures to be followed in the administration of the law (*procedural law*); and various kinds of criminal offenses (*criminal law*). Matters within public law often involve disputes where one of the parties represents the interests of "the people." The general idea is that some legal issues are such that the state, the community, or the people as a whole have a claim against one or more persons. Consider, for example, murder: when someone is charged with murder, it is not the victim (or friends or relatives thereof) who bring the case against the accused. Murder is an offense against the public order, an action that affects the interests of society as a whole. Thus, it is the state ("the people") who pursues charges against a defendant. This is what happened, for example, in the well-known case *The People of the State of California v. O. J. Simpson*—in the *public* trial of Simpson, charges were pursued by the Los Angeles County District Attorney's office representing the people of California, not just the deceased or their families.

II.1.2.2 Remedies and Penalties: Civil Law versus Criminal Law

Civil Law   The ideal behind civil law is that in some matters that are appropriately governed by the rules of the legal system, the legal finding that someone has acted inappropriately calls not for a legal *penalty,* but instead for a legal *remedy.* In civil law cases, the court is usually concerned with one party's claim that another party's actions have resulted in her being legally wronged ("damaged") in some way. If the court agrees that an injury has taken place, it acts to "right this legal wrong" by forcing the injurer to provide restitution designed to "repair" this damage and make the victim "whole" again (that is, as she was prior to the injury). For instance, if you were negligent in not shoveling the snow off your sidewalk and this caused the letter carrier to fall and injure himself, the letter carrier might file a civil suit against you in order to recover for his medical bills, lost wages, and even pain and suffering.

Criminal Law   This purportedly deals with actions and omissions that persons have a legal duty to perform or refrain from, and for which the appropriate response of the legal system to violations is the *criminal penalty.* The basic idea is that some actions demand that the legal system inflict punishment on those who perform them, as opposed to simply forcing them to "undo" the action that they have performed. Criminal law is typically designed to carve out the limits of legally permissible behavior, and criminal offenses are often offenses against public order. Again, in the O. J. Simpson criminal trial, the issue was not whether O. J. should be forced to compensate the families of his alleged victims, but instead whether he committed an act that merited the imposition of criminal penalties on him simply and precisely because of the nature of the committed act. In theory, the legal system reserves the criminal penalty for those acts that it considers the most serious violations of one's legal duties.

II.1.3 Torts and Contracts

Two of the most interesting areas of the law are *torts* and *contracts.* Each area typically merits a core first-year course in law school. They are also quite often the most challenging areas for beginning students to grasp. Though we cannot even begin to do justice to the complexities in either area, we provide in the following some helpful hints for dealing with the basics.

II.1.3.1 Torts

In our society, people have legal rights, and these include the right to their bodily security and the right to their property. Yet, these rights are often violated: people suffer injuries and losses at the hands of each other every day. It stands to reason that those who have been harmed as a result of a legal wrong committed by another person should be *compensated* for the injuries and/or losses they have suffered. This is where tort law comes in: the legal wrong in question need not involve a criminal offense, nor need it involve any issue for the public law. In order to show that a tort has occurred, one needs to show that a legal duty was breached, that the duty resulted in some kind of injury (typically to one's body or property), and that this injury merits compensation from the party who breached the legal duty.

Generally, torts fall into three major categories:

- Intentional torts
- Negligence
- Strict liability

Intentional Torts   There are several subcategories of intentional torts including trespass, defamation (*A* makes defamatory statements concerning *B* either in writing—*libel*—or orally—*slander*), assault and battery (*A* hits *B*), and false imprisonment. It is characteristic of all cases of intentional torts that the person who brings the lawsuit on account of having suffered harm (the *plaintiff*) claims that the person sued in the lawsuit (the *defendant*) either wanted the resultant harm or knew (with "substantial certainty") that the result would occur.

Negligence   In tort law, it is not always necessary to show that the defendant intended to cause the harm, or even intended to breach the duty, in order to show that a tort has been committed. The idea behind the tort of negligence is that each of us owes everyone in society a duty (specifically the duty of due care) to refrain from taking *unreasonable* risks associated with certain kinds of actions and omissions. And when such a risk is taken and injury is caused by our action, we have breached our duty of due care, and tort law requires that the injured party be compensated for her loss.

Clearly, *unreasonable conduct* resulting in injuries is the hallmark of the tort of negligence. Thus, we are not liable for every injury we cause, but only for those injuries that were the result of our conduct's falling below the standard of due care. The exact specification of the standard of due care in the law of negligence is a matter of protracted legal argument and beyond the scope of our present concerns.

Strict Liability   The so-called "strict-liability" torts involve narrow classes of action where the person performing the action is liable for harms he produces even if the harms are unintentional and could not have been prevented by exercising reasonable care. Strict liability is widely recognized in cases of injuries from "dangerous animals": an animal you possess attacks and injures someone; you are liable for the damages irrespective of your fault, negligence, or innocence. In Anglo-American law, strict liability has also been recognized in cases involving dangerous explosives. More recently, there appears to be a tendency to expand strict liability to cases involving injuries from manufactured goods (*products liability*).

II.1.3.2 Contracts

The domain of contract law is that of legally enforceable agreements among two or more parties. A contract is actually an agreement that involves the exchange of legal rights—for example, to money, property, one's labor, or even the right to be anywhere you want at a specific time—between the parties to a contract. Failure to perform one's part of the agreement can lead to a charge of *breach of contract,* for which a court can provide a remedy. It can force one party to do what the contract specifies, or it can award damages to the victim of the breach, which are usually calculated to bring the wronged party to a position equivalent to how things would have been had the contract not been breached.

Under what conditions are contracts valid? Generally speaking, legally enforceable contracts should meet all of the following necessary conditions:

- They should be entered into *voluntarily* by parties to them.
- The parties entering a contract must be *legally competent.*
- The terms of the contract must be *accurately represented* to the parties.

If these conditions are not met, the courts may not enforce the agreement. But in the case of a valid contract, each party has an enforceable legal claim against the other dictated by the terms of the contract. For example, suppose that when you go away on vacation, you pay a lawn-care company to take care of your property. When you return, all the grass is completely brown and all the bedding plants are dead. You ask your neighbors whether anyone came by to care for the lawn, and they say that they never saw anyone watering, fertilizing, or anything else. You should be able to get the courts to force the company to either put the grounds back the way they were before you left or pay you an amount at least equal to what it will cost you to find someone else to do it. If you had a valid contract with the lawn-care company, and if you can convince the court that their failure to perform caused the damage, they should be legally forced to provide you with a remedy.

II.1.3.3 Types of Liability in the Law

The foregoing discussion of torts and contracts suggests that there are different species of *legal liability*. For instance, liability for tortious injuries that we cause is one that the legal system imposes on us regardless of what we do—we do not assume it voluntarily. In contracts, however, our liability (for example, for breach of contract) is one that we have voluntarily assumed (duress usually invalidates a contract). The appropriate standard of liability varies according to the type of case in question. One set of distinctions among types of liability has to do with the state of mind of the person performing a specific act. Within certain areas of the law, it is said that "the act is not guilty unless the mind is guilty." Just what counts as a sufficiently "guilty mind" varies across legal contexts.

In some areas of the law (but not necessarily just the criminal law), the appropriate standard is *criminal liability*, according to which someone is liable if and only if it can be shown that the person was actually aware of the harmful or wrongful nature of his conduct. The most familiar instance of this standard is the requirement for murder that one not only kill a person, but do so with "*malice aforethought*." That is, unless it has been shown that the person was aware of the wrongful nature of his act, then the person is not guilty of murder. Similarly, fraud requires that a person engage in a deliberate misrepresentation, so that one must know that what one is saying is false, and intend to mislead another into believing that it is true. You would seem to be liable for fraud, for example, if you sold someone a house and said that you had a new roof installed last month, whereas you knew that the roof was more than ten years old. But you would not be guilty of fraud if you sold someone a car that, unbeknownst to you, had an alternator that was on the brink of failure.

In some areas of law, the appropriate standard is known as *objective liability*. To show that someone has violated this standard, one need not show any consciousness of harm or wrongdoing. Instead, one would need to show that *a reasonable person in relevantly similar circumstances would have been aware of the possibility of harm resulting from his act, or the wrongful nature of the act*. Suppose you ask your auto mechanic to check over the brakes of your older car prior to your taking it on an extended trip. Suppose now that during the trip your car's brakes fail due to a leak in the wheel cylinder; the car crashes, and there are personal injuries as well. The mechanic claims not to have been aware of any problem with the wheel cylinder, and did not think to check it out—he never even looked at it. But suppose you could prove that *a reasonable mechanic would have checked the entire braking system* on a car that old, especially given that he knew that you would be taking it on an extended trip. Then under the standard of objective liability, you would have shown that a reasonable person would have been aware of the dangers from failing to inspect the master cylinder, and thus you would have shown that your mechanic should be held liable in this case.

A third standard has come to be known as *strict liability*. According to this standard, one is liable if one causes harm, even if not only (i) there was no consciousness of wrongdoing by the party who caused the harm, but also

(ii) even a reasonable person would not have been aware of the possibility or harm resulting from the behavior. This is a very controversial standard of liability that gained greater acceptance and assumed a broader scope in the twentieth century. At present, strict liability operates in only a few areas of the law, and applies only in cases where certain conditions are met. We will not go into those conditions here. For us the important point to note is how it differs from the other conceptions discussed earlier. Two familiar examples of the strict liability standard come from the criminal law. Both statutory rape and bigamy are criminal offenses where strict liability holds. If one has sex with an underage partner or one marries again while still married, it does not matter whether one was unaware of one's wrongdoing or even whether a reasonable person would not have been aware of it either. If one performs the act, one is liable; this is the mark of strict liability.

Excuses and *Mens Rea*

The careful reader will have figured out that the idea of a *legal excuse* is closely related to these respective conceptions of liability. For example, if a case is governed by criminal liability, then even if a defendant has caused harm to another, he can offer as an excuse that he was not aware of the possibility of harm resulting from his action. Likewise, if the standard is objective liability, a defendant can evade the charge even if he caused the harm in question if he can demonstrate that not only was he unaware of the possibility of harm but also that a reasonable person in relevantly similar circumstances would not have been aware of the possibility of harm either. On the other hand, if a case turns on the issue of strict liability, no such excuse will do—if his behavior caused the harm, then he is liable.

Another closely related concept is that of *mens rea,* which translates literally from the Latin as "mental thing." We might render it more colloquially as "state of mind." The careful reader will already have surmised that the principal differences among strict, objective, and criminal liability lie in the claims about the state of mind that must be satisfied according to each standard. Strict liability carries no *mens rea* requirement—showing liability does not require showing anything about the state of mind of the defendant or anyone else. Objective liability does not require showing anything about the defendant's actual state of mind, but it does require showing that a reasonable person would have had some particular state of mind (awareness of the possibility of harm or wrongdoing). So it is fair to say that objective liability relies on a hypothetical or counterfactual *mens rea* requirement. Criminal liability has the strictest *mens rea* requirement, that the defendant must be shown to have possessed some specific mental state— awareness of the harmful (or wrongful) nature of his conduct.

II.2 THE STRUCTURE OF THE AMERICAN LEGAL SYSTEM

In this section, we briefly examine two core features of the American legal system, namely, the doctrine of separation of powers and the structure of the court system.

II.2.1 Separation of Powers and the Branches of Government

Separation of Powers   The so-called *separation of powers* doctrine lies at the heart of the structure of the American system of government. The basics of the doctrine include the claims that (a) state powers can be divided into a relatively small set of *distinct* functions or elements, and (b) one can structure a system of government in such a way that these distinct powers can be divided up so that *different* people possess each of them. The central idea of the doctrine is that of a balanced system of government: the various powers within a system of government should be fenced off from each other in order to ensure that not all political power is concentrated in the hands of one individual or set of individuals (as it was the case, for example, with the *Politburo* in the former Soviet Union).

The doctrine has its roots in the great political thinkers of the Enlightenment, most notably the French philosopher Montesquieu and the British philosopher John Locke, although it can also be found in the writings of the Renaissance political thinker Niccolo Machiavelli.

In the United States, the separation of powers is so familiar to most American citizens that we hardly ever think about it in any careful analytic way. We simply assume it as a fundamental tenet of the way our legal system is structured. Yet given that the importance of the doctrine can hardly be overemphasized, we should take a moment to recall the basics of the doctrine.

Federalism and the Bill of Rights

Notice that the separation of powers according to the *function* of government is but one way of dividing power within the American Constitution. An alternative way, also incorporated in the Constitution, is *federalism,* a system in which power is divided up on a *geographical basis*. The guiding idea is that the power of the central government (that is, the federal government) needs to be constrained by regional governments that enjoy some degree of autonomy. Finally, power is also divided up between the government and the private citizens when our Constitution incorporates a *bill of rights*—a list of basic, inalienable rights of citizens that government cannot violate.

The Constitution of the United States contains a number of provisions that spell out exactly how various powers of the state are to be distributed. In short, it recognizes three distinct functions within our system of government:

- making law—legislative function
- enforcing law—executive function
- interpreting/applying law—judicial function

These three distinct functions are assigned respectively to the legislative, executive, and judicial branches of the government.

The Legislative Branch   It should hardly be surprising that the role of the legislature is to make laws. The standard way that laws come into existence in the American legal system is for a bill to be introduced in one of the houses of Congress. The members of Congress then vote on the bill, and if a majority in each house votes in favor of the bill, it is sent to the president for his signature. The president can sign the bill, at which point it becomes law, or can veto the bill. (But in the event of a veto, the legislative branch can "override" the veto if a two-thirds majority of each house votes to override, at which point the bill would become law.) Notice that the president does not get to vote on legislation, nor (in theory) does the president get to introduce legislation (so-called "presidential bills" are technically introduced by a friendly member of the House or Senate). Notice also that the Congress has no power of law enforcement, nor does it determine whether a violation of law has occurred (except for rare instances such as impeachment).

The Executive Branch   This includes the president, vice president, and the various departments that make up the "cabinet" and its subsidiaries. This branch has the nominal duty of enforcing the law. The president acts as the commander-in-chief of the Armed Forces, the Justice Department pursues certain violations of federal law, the State Department conducts foreign policy (allegedly within the bounds of laws created by Congress), the Internal Revenue Service (IRS) collects income taxes, and so forth. Although certain agencies within the executive branch do have the power to make policy on certain issues (for example, the Food and Drug Administration), their power usually has resulted from a piece of legislation that specifically empowered them to do so (for example, the Food, Drug and Cosmetics Act of 1906). The executive branch does not normally possess the power to determine when a violation of law has occurred, nor can it determine punishments for those found to have violated the law.

The Judicial Branch   The judicial branch is charged with applying and interpreting the law. This branch of the federal government includes the various federal district courts, appeals courts, and the Supreme Court, which is the highest court in the system. In addition to judges, it also includes various federal district attorneys and prosecutors, whose job includes determining if there is good reason to believe that violations have occurred, and presenting the "government's" case if a trial results. Overall, the application of the law is the judiciary's primary function, which includes determining punishments when it finds that a violation has occurred.

It is important to note that the judicial branch does not have the power to make law, nor does it have the power to enforce the law—these are functions assigned to the other branches of the legal system. Indeed, the fundamental idea of the doctrine of separation of powers is that each branch is independent of the others, and no government official can belong to more than one branch at a time. But this brings up the question "What happens if a branch of government abuses its power?"

The answer is to be found in an idea closely related to that of the separation of powers (indeed, often indistinguishable from it), namely, the idea of *checks and balances*. According to this notion, in addition to the explicit functions assigned to each branch, there is the implicit function of providing a check on possible misconduct on the part of one of the other branches. In theory, if one branch were to engage in tyranny, the other two would be required to combat this tyranny by legal means. Suppose, for example, Congress passed a law requiring that children be given religious instruction in the public schools. Given the First Amendment's prohibition of the "establishment" of religion, we should expect the Supreme Court to exercise its power of *judicial review* of this law in order to put a "check" on this congressional action and declare the law invalid if it violates the Constitution. In this way, the types of power allocated to the three branches function as a barrier to tyrannical uses of power by any branch. Clearly the most important implications for, and questions about, the separation of powers are those that concern political philosophy. For instance, if (as political philosophers do) we ask the question "What type of governmental structure provides the best safeguard against tyranny?" our discussion might focus on the issue of how well this structure does so, and compare it with other attempts to build such safeguards into the structure of a legal system. As the popular contemporary slogan asserts, judges are not supposed to "legislate from the bench." But suppose, in an example that is deliberately fanciful, that Congress passed a law prohibiting anyone from doing anything that offended any judge. Now could judges apply this law and still succeed in refraining from "legislating from the bench"? One argument might go roughly like this: The problem in this case is that even though the rule against offending judges technically originated in the legislative branch, the law is so vague and indeterminate that people cannot have any idea what it requires and prohibits. Judges would in fact be making the law in the sense that *they* would determine what is and is not against the law—judges, not legislators, would be determining what citizens' legal obligations are. The moral of the story is that in order to maintain the separation of powers, laws must not only originate in the legislature, but they must be crafted in such a way to rule out judges actually making law in the process of applying law. We will see shortly just how important this is.

II.2.2 The Court System

In general, courts exist in order to resolve disputes that arise between different people or legal entities. The resolution of disputes is achieved by the courts when they apply the law to specific controversies brought before them in an impartial and fair way.

The court system in the United States contains many subdivisions, some of which overlap. The first thing to be noted is that in the United States, we have *two* systems of courts: *federal courts* and *state courts.* Federal courts hear cases that involve matters such as constitutional issues, the application and interpretation of federal statutes, interstate commerce, and rulings of federal agencies. Other issues are typically dealt with under some wing of the court systems of individual states, which also include county and municipal courts. Areas such as family law, claims of breach of contract, and damages due to negligence by an individual typically are decided within state courts. Although these questions of jurisdiction are often complex, and are generally addressed in law-school classes on civil and criminal procedure, a handy rule of thumb would hold that a case will generally go to a state (or county or municipal) court unless it directly raises a constitutional issue, involves a matter that concerns more than one state, or deals with an issue over which the federal government has assumed jurisdiction (for example, anti-trust).

A different kind of distinction among courts concerns the way courts are organized in a hierarchical way: at the lower level are the *trial courts* where cases first start, while at the higher level we find various *appellate courts* whose function is to review the work of lower courts.

The Federal Court System

United States Supreme Court
- Highest appellate court in the land
- Hears appeals from the U.S. courts of appeals and from the highest level appellate court in each state (on issues involving federal law)
- Leave to appeal is limited and must be granted by the court

United States Court of Appeals
- Intermediate appellate court
- Divided into thirteen courts consisting of twelve regional circuits and the Court of Appeals for the Federal Circuit
- Hears appeals from the U.S. district courts, Bankruptcy Court, U.S. Tax Court, and administrative agency tribunals
- Automatic right to appeal

United States District Court
- Trial court
- Divided into ninety-four regional districts
- Has original jurisdiction over the following cases:
  —Criminal cases involving violation of federal statutes
  —Civil cases requiring a determination of rights under federal law
  —Diversity of citizenship cases (civil cases involving plaintiffs from two or more states and the amount in controversy exceeds $50,000)

II.2.2.1 Trial Courts

Most disputes never make it to trial. The great majority of civil lawsuits are resolved by a mutual agreement (*settlement*) between the parties. Similarly, only a mere 10 percent of criminal cases ever go to trial—about 90 percent of criminal cases are either ended by a guilty plea or are dismissed. Nonetheless, when a case goes to trial, the function of the trial court is to act as an impartial third party that allows the adversaries in a dispute to present their case for judgment. Thus, in general, during a trial in a court of law, the facts and the law(s) governing the facts are first determined, then the law is applied to the facts, and finally the dispute is resolved by the judgment of the court.

There are numerous kinds of trial courts both at the federal and the state level, and the limits of their authority to try a case (*jurisdiction*) vary from court to court. (In general, we distinguish two kinds of courts: courts of *limited jurisdiction,* for example, "traffic courts," and courts of *general jurisdiction,* which try either criminal or civil cases with no upper bound on the penalties or remedies involved.) Trial courts generally deal with two sorts of issues: questions of fact and questions of law. Sometimes parties disagree about what events have taken place, for instance, whether an auto mechanic's negligence caused the failure of the brakes that caused a collision which caused property and bodily damage, or whether O. J. Simpson killed Nicole Brown and Ronald Goldman. Other times the parties agree on the facts but disagree about how the law applies to those facts, as when a husband admits that he struck his wife but claims that it is not a case of battery. Quite often, however, parties disagree about both questions of fact and questions of law. Suppose, for example, an auto mechanic claims that he was not negligent in performing repairs on an automobile, that it was the driver's inattentiveness that caused the collision, and that since the owner signed a document absolving the mechanic from liability (perhaps the mechanic recommended that the braking system be replaced, but the owner agreed only to limited repairs), he should not be held liable even if brake failure had caused the collision. Verdicts by trial courts can be rendered by the judge who hears the case or by a jury, if a party invokes the so-called right to a jury trial. But in either case, the verdict of a trial court can involve a finding of fact, an application of the law to a set of facts, or both.

Trial courts are the courts most familiar to the average person. Indeed, as Hollywood and TV depict them, trial courts are places of high drama: reluctant witnesses are examined and "torn apart" by devious lawyers; "shattering" evidence is introduced; and "legal eagles" make dramatic appeals and arguments to the jury. In reality, however, trial courts are not quite as glamorous: numerous formal and technical procedures must be followed; records must be kept; and language and arguments used must be restrained to conform to exact rules of procedure.

II.2.2.2 Appeals Courts

Once a verdict has been delivered by a trial court, the parties to the dispute retain the right to file an appeal, which is an argument challenging the trial court's verdict (though most states recognize only the defendant's right to appeal

Burden of Proof and Legal Presumption

The legal conception of *burden of proof* is closely related to another legal conception, that of a *legal presumption*. Here is basically how each works. Consider a *criminal* proceeding in which a defendant is accused of committing arson. The state will attempt to prove *beyond a reasonable doubt* that the defendant committed the crime. In this proceeding, there is a *presumption that the defendant is innocent*, which means that the court will begin the proceeding with the initial presupposition that the defendant is not guilty, and the state has the burden of convincing the court that the defendant did indeed commit the crime. So it is not just that the court assumes a position of neutrality about the defendant's guilt (that is, neither guilty nor innocent), in which case all the prosecution would have to do is sway it sufficiently from this neutral position; instead, the state has the burden of convincing the court, which begins with the presumption that the defendant did not do it.

Things are different in *civil* cases. In a civil case—say, a case involving a claim of breach of contract—the court is not predisposed to believe that there was or that there was not a breach. The jury is normally instructed to decide from the *preponderance of the evidence* whether one of the competing accounts in the trial is more *probably* true. The presumption of innocence is rebuttable in the sense that the prosecution can make a case that overcomes it, but to prevail, the prosecution must succeed in rebutting it.

in criminal cases). As you might expect, the appeal is filed with an appeals court, whose function is to consider arguments to the effect that the trial court has issued a mistaken judgment. Appeals courts generally mimic the jurisdictional structure outlined for trial courts—federal appeals courts generally hear appeals of judgments of federal courts, and state appeals courts hear appeals of state court judgments (county and municipal appeals are usually directed to state appeals courts). However, there is one major exception: if in an appeal a criminal defendant argues that a state court (trial or appeals) has somehow mishandled a major federal issue, such as the First Amendment's right to free speech, a case that began in a state court can end up in a federal appeals court for adjudication of the federal issue raised by the case.

Most appeals are based on the claim that there was a procedural error(s) during the trial and/or errors in the judge's interpretation of the law. This points to one significant difference between trial and appeals courts: although one typical function of a trial court is to determine the legally relevant facts, this is generally not what appeals courts do. In fact, appeals courts generally take as given the judgment of the trial court on the facts of the case (if, indeed, facts were in dispute), and instead confine themselves to *matters of law*. One of the only times that an appeals court will get involved in the fact-finding process is if the appeal claims that some rule of evidence was violated by the trial court. And even there, the issue is (strictly speaking) a matter of law, since it is a rule of evidence that is in question. So since it is fair to say that appeals courts generally confine themselves to matters of law, it would also appear that a successful appeal not only must claim that the trial court's ultimate judgment was mistaken, but it also must find some error in the application of the law that led the trial court to its mistaken verdict. (Not all errors of law are cause for reversal of the decision of the trial court: an error might be a *harmless error,* an error minor enough to not disturb the fair nature of the trial; to be a *reversible error,* the error must be determined to be harmful to the fairness of the trial.)

The process by which one pursues an appeal is worthy of note. The appealing party is the *appellant* or *petitioner,* and the other party in the dispute is the *appellee* or *respondent.* The appellant must petition the appeals court to issue a *writ of certiorari* which, if granted, instructs the lower court to forward its record of the case to the court issuing the writ. We should point out that most petitions are not granted; consequently, most requests for an appeal do not succeed. It is pretty much up to the appeals court to decide whether it will hear an appeal from a litigant.

If an appeal is granted, both the appellant and the appellee present the court with *briefs,* written arguments containing their side's view of the legal facts (that is, matters of law); and the court has a choice of deciding the case on the basis of the briefs alone or asking that the case be scheduled for *oral arguments.* When the court makes a judgment about the appeal, it sometimes (although certainly not all the time) issues a written judgment in which it lays out the reasons for deciding the case in the way that it did. Such written documents are referred to as the legal *opinions* of the appeals court. But here the word *opinion* should not be understood to connote something like the "purely subjective and arbitrary feelings" of the judges of the appeals court—legal opinions are arguments designed to demonstrate that one legal result is entailed by the law itself (and perhaps the facts of the case). So legal opinions are not purely conjectural matters; they are paradigm cases of *reasoning within the law*—arguments that there is one legally correct result in this specific case. The opinions of appellate courts are of focal interest from the perspective of reasoning in the law; thus, we examine the issues involved here in more detail in chapter 4 and in part III of this book.

II.2.2.3 The Supreme Court
We have seen that a litigant has the legal right to pursue an appeal of a court's judgment on a matter of law. But a little reflection should reveal that this process cannot go on forever—there must be a point beyond which there is no further appeal, that is, a point where the court's decision is final. In the American legal system, this point is represented by the *Supreme Court.* The Supreme Court of the United States is the "highest court in the land"; it is specifically designated as such by the Constitution, and it is a coequal institution with the presidency and the Congress. Once a case has reached the Supreme Court and the Court issues a judgment on it, then that case is settled once and for all.

The Court is presided over by nine justices (six must be present for a quorum, and at least four must vote to grant full review of a case), and it has two sorts of jurisdiction: *appellate* and *original.* The *appellate jurisdiction* of the Court is defined by the Congress, which over the years has passed laws increasingly widening the range of cases for possible review. The *original jurisdiction* of the Court, the cases it alone can try, is set by the Constitution itself. In general, the great bulk of the cases reviewed by the Court belong to its appellate jurisdiction. Like other appeals courts, the Supreme Court receives and considers petitions from litigants whose cases have usually made their way through lower courts. The Supreme Court also rejects most petitions for certiorari, and most of the time does so without comment. (During recent years, the Court has been hearing approximately 100 cases per term on the average out of the thousands it is asked to review each year.) But the Court also publishes its opinions, which are often important legal arguments regarding landmark cases and, as such, occupy an important place in the legal system. Every court in the U.S. must follow the Supreme Court on matters of law, so that if a lower court decision appears to conflict with a Supreme Court decision, the latter always wins out. And since all other courts must defer to and follow the decisions of the Supreme Court, the arguments within its published opinions are among the most important documents within the legal system.

FOR FURTHER
READING

INTRODUCTIONS TO LOGIC AND REASONING

Copi, Irving M., and Carl Cohen. *Introduction to Logic.* 8th ed. New York: Macmillan Publishing, 1990.

Fogelin, Robert J. *Understanding Arguments: An Introduction to Informal Logic.* 5th ed. Fort Worth, TX: Harcourt Brace, 1997.

Gustason, William. *Reasoning from Evidence: Inductive Logic,* New York: Macmillan Publishing, 1994.

Hurley, Patrick J. *A Concise Introduction to Logic.* 3d ed. Belmont, CA: Wadsworth Publishing, 1988.

Kahane, Howard. *Logic and Contemporary Rhetoric: The Use of Reason in Everyday Life.* 3d ed. Belmont, CA: Wadsworth Publishing, 1980.

Moore, Brooke Noel, and Richard Parker. *Critical Thinking.* 4th ed. Mountain View, CA: Mayfield Publishing, 1995.

Nosich, Gerald M. *Reasons and Arguments.* Belmont, CA: Wadsworth Publishing, 1982.

Runkle, Gerald. *Good Thinking: An Introduction to Logic.* 3d ed. Austin, TX: Holt, Rinehart & Winston, 1991.

Scriven, Michael. *Reasoning.* New York: McGraw-Hill, 1976.

Thomas, Stephen Naylor. *Practical Reasoning in Natural Language.* 3d ed. Englewood Cliffs, NJ: Prentice-Hall, 1986.

Toulmin, Steven, Richard Rieke, and Allan Janik. *An Introduction to Reasoning.* 2d ed. New York: Macmillan Publishing, 1984.

INTRODUCTIONS TO THE LAW

Fletcher, George P. *Basic Concepts of Legal Thought.* Oxford: Oxford University Press, 1996.

Golding, Martin P. *Philosophy of Law.* Englewood Cliffs, NJ: Prentice-Hall, 1975.

Honore, Tony. *About Law: An Introduction.* Oxford: Clarendon Press, 1995.

Murphy, Jeffrie G., and Jules L. Coleman. *Philosophy of Law: An Introduction to Jurisprudence.* Rev. ed. Boulder, CO: Westview Press, 1990.

Pincoffs, Edmund L. *Philosophy of Law: A Brief Introduction.* Belmont, CA: Wadsworth Publishing, 1991.

Post, C. Gordon. *An Introduction to the Law.* Englewood Cliffs, NJ: Prentice-Hall, 1963.

ANTHOLOGIES ON LAW

Altman, Andrew. *Arguing About Law: An Introduction to Legal Philosophy.* 2d ed. Belmont, CA: Wadsworth Publishing, 2000.

d'Amato, Anthony. *Analytic Jurisprudence Anthology.* Cincinnati, OH: Anderson Publishing, 1996.

Feinberg, Joel, and Hyman Gross. *Philosophy of Law.* 6th ed. Belmont, CA: Wadsworth Publishing, 1995.

Hanks, Eva H., Michael E. Herz, and Steven S. Nemerson. *Elements of Law.* Cincinnati, OH: Anderson Publishing, 1994.

Schauer, Frederick, and Walter Sinnott-Armstrong. *The Philosophy of Law: Classic and Contemporary Readings with Commentary.* Fort Worth, TX: Harcourt Brace, 1996.

Smith, Patricia. *The Nature and Process of Law: An Introduction to Legal Philosophy.* Oxford: Oxford University Press, 1993.

White, Jefferson, and Dennis Patterson. *Introduction to the Philosophy of Law: Readings and Cases.* Oxford: Oxford University Press, 1999.

LEGAL REASONING TEXTS
Introductory/Intermediate

Burton, Steven J. *An Introduction to Law and Legal Reasoning.* 2d ed. New York: Little, Brown, 1995.

Levi, Edward H. *An Introduction to Legal Reasoning.* Chicago: University of Chicago Press, 1949.

Vandevelde, Kenneth J. *Thinking Like a Lawyer: An Introduction to Legal Reasoning.* Boulder, CO: Westview Press, 1998.

Advanced

Alexy, Robert. *A Theory of Legal Argumentation: The Theory of Rational Discourse as Theory of Legal Justification.* Oxford: Clarendon Press, 1989.

Golding, M.P. *Legal Reasoning.* New York: Alfred A. Knopf, 1984.

Kolodner, J. *Case Based Reasoning.* Los Altos, CA: Morgan Kaufmann, 1993.

Levin, Joel. *How Judges Reason: The Logic of Adjudication.* New York: Peter Lang Publishing, 1992.

MacCormick, Neil. *Legal Reasoning and Legal Theory.* Oxford: Clarendon Press, 1978.

Wasserstrom, R. A. *The Judicial Decision—Towards a Theory of Legal Justification.* Stanford: Stanford University Press, 1961.

Zelermyer, William. *The Process of Legal Reasoning.* Englewood Cliffs, NJ: Prentice-Hall, 1960.

USEFUL GUIDES ON ANALYTICAL/ ARGUMENTATIVE WRITING

Bedau, Hugo. *Thinking and Writing About Philosophy.* Boston: Bedford Books of St. Martin's Press, 1996.

Martinich, A. P. Philosophical Writing. 2d ed. Malden, MA: Blackwell Publishers, 1996.

Moore, Brooke Noel. *Making Your Case: Critical Thinking and the Argumentative Essay.* Mountain View, CA: Mayfield Publishing, 1995.

Seech, Zachary. *Writing Philosophy Papers.* Belmont, CA: Wadsworth Publishing, 1993.

Stramel, James S. *How to Write a Philosophy Paper.* New York: University Press of America, 1995.